Benedict XVI

Benedict XVI

COMMANDER OF THE FAITH

RUPERT SHORTT

Hodder & Stoughton

British Library Cataloguing in Publication Data
A record for this book is available from the British Library

ISBN 0 340 86429 X

Typeset in Baskerville by Avon DataSet Ltd,
Bidford-on-Avon, Warwickshire

Printed and bound in Great Britain by
Clays Ltd, St Ives plc

The paper used in this book is a natural recyclable product
made from wood grown in sustainable forests.
The hard coverboard is recycled.

Hodder & Stoughton
A Division of Hodder Headline Ltd
338 Euston Road
London NW1 3BH
www.madaboutbooks.com

For Lucy Lethbridge

Contents

Acknowledgements

For inviting me to write a concise biography of Pope Benedict XVI within a few months of his election, I am most grateful to Judith Longman of Hodder. She and her colleagues have done much to ease a hefty burden along the way. Warm thanks are also due to my interviewees in Europe, Latin America and the United States: James Alison, Dr Tina Beattie, Professor Wolfgang Beinert, Professor Charles Curran, Daniel Deckers, Fr Augustine Di Noia OP, Fr Joseph Fessio SJ, Professor Mark Francis CSV, Fr Thomas Frauenlob, Dom Manel Gasch, Bishop Christopher Hill, Professor Werner Jeanrond, the Revd John Kennedy, Professor Nicholas Lash, Fr Daniel Madigan SJ, Fr Martin Maier SJ, Professor David Martin, Fr Richard Neuhaus, Fr Aidan Nichols OP, Fr Robert Nugent SDS, Professor Gerald O'Collins SJ, Professor Keith Pecklers SJ, Francis Pimentel-Pinto, Dr John Pollard, Fr Timothy Radcliffe OP, Fr John Rock SJ, Dr Perry Schmidt-Leukel, Abbot Jeremias Schröder, Professor Christoph Schwöbel, Fr Geoffrey Steel, Marta Villanueva, Dom Henry Wansbrough, Archbishop Rowan Williams, Abbot Notker Wolf and Dom Eduardo Zamarro.

The Benedictine community at Sant'Anselmo in Rome were marvellous hosts during the aftermath of the conclave. So, too, were the staff of St Cuthman's retreat centre in Sussex. Practical help of other forms was kindly given by Tom Shortt, Robert Mickens, Robert Nowell, José Prado, Sarah Hillman, Broo Doherty, Alex Blasdel and Dom Henry O'Shea. Four people – Glyn Paflin, Fr Peter Cornwell, Dr John Page and Professor Joseph Komonchak SJ – read the manuscript in whole or in part, and suggested a large number of improvements. The remaining flaws are of course my own.

Finally, I am deeply indebted to Christa Pongratz-Lippitt, for her very painstaking guidance on church affairs in the German-speaking world; to my former colleagues John Whale and Christopher Herdon, for no less valuable advice on broader matters; and to Iga Downing, who has done more than anyone to help me recover my health after the back injury I suffered in 1997.

Rupert Shortt
September 2005

Introduction

This book is a condensed chronicle that makes no claim to being comprehensive. My aim, rather, is to trace some of the main strands in the Pope's life and thought, and thus to help cast light on a mystery. Biographers regularly voice well-founded unease about headline reports on their subjects. Dr Rowan Williams, for example, was unsubtly labelled by parts of the press as a liberal when he became Archbishop of Canterbury in 2002. Benedict XVI's case is different. The familiar descriptions of him can seem discordant: he has been called wise, gentle and kind, a strict and sometimes harsh enforcer, a lofty mind, and a champion of simple believers. But none of these epithets is inaccurate. The velvet glove and the iron fist are both authentic.

Perhaps the biggest question facing a commentator on Joseph Ratzinger's career is why he renounced the liberal instincts that made him a champion of reform at the Second Vatican Council (1962–65) for the ardent conservatism that marked his long tenure as Prefect of the Congregation for the Doctrine of the Faith. The evolution is remarkable. In 1962, he was calling on the powers that be to ventilate an airless room: 'What the Church needs today as always are not adulators to extol the status quo, but men whose humility and obedience are not less than their passion for the truth . . .' Instead, he went on, a monolithic institution was 'entrenching herself behind exterior safeguards'.[1] But by the mid-1980s, he was arguing that 'the damage we have incurred in these twenty years is due . . . to the unleashing within the Church of latent polemical and centrifugal forces', and outside the Church to threats posed by a 'liberal-radical ideology of individualistic, rationalistic and hedonistic stamp'.[2] The hard-line message was restated in his address to fellow cardinals just before the 2005 conclave. Rejecting what he termed the 'dictatorship of relativism' in Western society, he went on to denounce those who regarded 'clear faith' as 'fundamentalism'.

The pages ahead will have a good deal to report on matters of practical concern to Christians and others, including ethics, liturgy, ecumenism, interfaith dialogue, and the bonds between religion and politics. At the outset, though, it is worth looking beneath the topsoil of church affairs at Benedict's intellectual roots. Moves to the theological Right are sometimes portrayed in terms of a development from adherence to St Thomas Aquinas, understood as seeing a generous diffusion of divine grace in the world, towards a vision more influenced by St Augustine, who is pictured as less optimistic about secular culture, and yoked to a theology of the cross. Whether thinkers as sophisticated as Augustine and Aquinas can be pigeon-holed in this way is questionable, but it is easy to recognise the outlooks ascribed to them.

In the West, at least, the major Christian denominations have always witnessed intermittent debates between those who believe that the Church must avert its gaze from a sinful world, and others who favour a more open-handed interaction with culture. Nineteenth- and early twentieth-century Roman Catholicism was a case in point. For 200 years after the Enlightenment, the Church famously resembled a well-defended castle. It pulled up its drawbridge on modernity, condemning extensions of the franchise, women's rights, scientific developments and biblical scholarship. Pope Pius IX, who helped usher in the doctrine of papal infallibility at the First Vatican Council in 1869–70, had earlier rejected the proposition that 'the Roman Pontiff can and ought to reconcile . . . himself with progress, liberalism and modern civilisation'. Pius X's reign from 1903 to 1914 saw a further repudiation of contemporary thought, and the introduction of an oath obliging all clergy to uphold an ultra-traditionalist interpretation of the faith.

It was not ever thus. Among many examples of a protean resourcefulness, the Church had absorbed and reinterpreted the prevailing Platonist philosophy during the second, third and fourth centuries, and had reached a similar accommodation with Aristotelianism in the Middle Ages. Before condemning Galileo, it had jettisoned biblical cosmology in favour of a Greek model, based on the movement of the spheres. In the late twentieth century, John Paul II became a notable champion of democracy. Much of Pius IX's defensiveness was part of an after-shock from the French Revolution and the loss of the papal states during the Risorgimento. *Gaudium et Spes* ('Joy and Hope'), the Second Vatican Council's Pastoral Constitution on the Church and the Modern World, recovered a long-dormant tradition of Christian humanism: 'The joys and hopes, the griefs and anxieties of the men and women of this age, especially those who are poor or in any way afflicted, these too are the joys and hopes, the griefs and anxieties of the followers of Christ. Indeed, nothing genuinely human fails to raise an echo in their hearts.'

Even at the time, Ratzinger entertained private doubts about the mindset underlying parts of this document. With hindsight, he and others (including the then Archbishop Karol Wojtyla) began to wonder whether the Church hadn't embraced the world just as the world was moving in another direction. Ratzinger's impression was confirmed by what struck him as the excesses of the *soixantehuitards*, and, his friends say, by guilt at his own part in releasing a liberal genie from the bottle.

So his shift of view was less abrupt than is commonly supposed (and in any case, Augustine's thought has always attracted him far more than Thomas's). It is also vital to grasp that discussion at Vatican II was not marked by a simple liberal–conservative split. The theological Left consisted of a tactical alliance embracing devotees of *aggiornamento* – bringing the Church up to date – and of *ressourcement* – the impulse to energise contemporary discussion by a re-engagement with Christian origins. During the 1940s and 50s, *ressourcement*-minded Catholics joined in calls to eschew the perceived tyranny of Pius XII and his immediate predecessors. But their battle-cry was based less on keeping up with the times than on an urge to recover an ancient model of the Church. This model was profoundly sacramental, and more concerned with organic communion than institutional structure. Ratzinger belonged to the *ressourcement* camp, as became clearer after the mid-60s, when the forces for change effectively splintered.

Among the consequences of this fragmentation was a shift in the terms of the debate. By the late 1960s, the erstwhile allies were talking more about how to understand human nature than about church government as such; and they tended to divide along the 'Augustinian'/'Thomist' lines I have already sketched. The dispute's theological kernel is how grace and nature relate.

3

Does grace draw out the best in human nature, crown it, bring it to fulfilment? Or does it radically burrow down inside believers, and remake them from the bottom up? This question was crystallised in a clash between two of the twentieth century's foremost Catholic thinkers, the existentialist Karl Rahner and the neo-orthodox Hans Urs von Balthasar. For von Balthasar, as for a Protestant titan such as Karl Barth, grace has to flatten before it rebuilds. For Rahner, grace is the blossoming of material already present in humanity. Ratzinger would gravitate towards von Balthasar and away from Rahner, his former mentor and friend, during the 1970s.

What are the implications of this perhaps arcane-sounding debate? The subject of a Christian's right relation to the world was once broached more directly by the journalist and historian Paul Johnson in *The Spectator*. He condemned an editorial in *The Tablet* which suggested that the Catholic Church should do more to commend itself to the modern world. The 'modern world', argued Johnson,

> is Freud, Hitler and Stalin. It is Auschwitz and the gulag, it is AIDS and anorexia, crack and speed, Hiroshima and the killing fields, San Francisco bath houses and Bangkok child brothels. At its miserable best it is downmarket tabloids, Disneyland and Channel 4 soft porn. At its worst it is human degradation so complete and cruelty so heartless as to leave Satan and his pandemonium gasping with pride at their creation . . . The last thing the Catholic Church ought to do is to commend itself to such a world and those who accept its culture. It is the task of Catholicism to fight the modern world, to defy it, excoriate it, expose its shams and lies, its follies and meanness and frauds.[3]

The Tablet's then Editor, Wilkins, was unpersuaded by this. Conservative certainties 'have their appeal', he wrote in reply. 'But Pope John XXIII rang down the curtain on the Disapproving Church. [The Council Fathers] made an act of trust in the Spirit in the world and in the People of God, and there is no going back.'[4] Wilkins's comment will seem fair to many; but Johnson's view is closer to Pope Benedict's. Before his election, Cardinal Ratzinger said several times that the Church's heyday lies in the past, and that Western society is undergoing a return to paganism reminiscent of the Dark Ages. He also pointed out that sombre estimates of human nature have a theological pedigree long predating Augustine, let alone the Reformation. The Old Testament speaks of a righteous remnant amid an ungodly multitude, and Jesus himself echoed this idea many times, especially with his teaching on the 'little flock' in Luke 12.

So it is not only liberals who have felt embattled over recent decades. From the late 1960s onwards, Ratzinger began insisting on the need for ceaseless vigilance against the temptation to make the faith easy or palatable. The preface of his *Introduction to Christianity*[5] illustrates the point with the parable called 'Honest Jack'. A man carrying a burdensome lump of gold exchanged it successively for a horse, a cow, a goose and a whetstone, 'which he finally threw into the water without losing much; on the contrary, what he now gained in exchange, so he thought, was the precious gift of complete freedom.' For Ratzinger, this tale is a warning to theologians drawing ever closer to secular norms, and offering the rest of society less and less in which to disbelieve in consequence. Add together beliefs about the truth of Christianity and the concealment of this truth by sin, and it is not hard to see the inference many might draw: that discipleship is more about duties than rights, and a global Church must be subject to strong central controls.

These arguments should in turn be seen against the background of Ratzinger's thinking about conscience. In an important address on the subject to American bishops in 1991,[6] he questioned 'the opposition of authority to subjectivity', and the fashion for seeing conscience as a purely internal mechanism. What is called the voice of conscience may simply be a reflection of the social surroundings and 'opinions in vogue', he said. Whether something is recognised as true or not also depends on the will, which can either block or unblock the discernment process. So good judgement is dependent on 'an already formed moral character which can either continue to deform or be further purified'.

He concluded that the middle term establishing the connection between authority and subjectivity is truth. For this reason, Ratzinger was happy to endorse Cardinal Newman's famous remark that he would drink a toast to conscience first, and then to the Pope, because the centrality of conscience to Newman is linked to the prior centrality of truth. 'The Pope cannot impose commandments on faithful Catholics because he wants to or finds it expedient', Ratzinger continued. 'Such a modern, voluntaristic concept of authority can only distort the true theological meaning of the papacy. The true nature of the Petrine office has become so incomprehensible in the modern age no doubt because we only think of authority in terms which do not allow for bridges between subject and object.' In other words, the contemporary world is disfigured by relativism. With the discrediting of Marxism's claim to truth, Ratzinger maintains, disbelief in truth as such now ranks as the greatest intellectual hazard of all. He has repeated this message in public debates with atheist intellectuals such as Jürgen Habermas and Paolo Flores d'Arcais.

Benedict XVI is by some margin the most distinguished thinker to occupy Peter's chair in at least a century, perhaps much longer. Even if he were not a very fine theologian, it would not be my business to offer categorical verdicts on complex debates about authority, the limits of diversity, and the relation between form and content in Christian preaching. But at least four points have been made which may serve to circumscribe the Pope's publicly expressed view. First, although his insights into the workings of conscience are penetrating, he fails to reckon sufficiently with the implications of past mistakes. The Church has regularly sought to bind the consciences of the faithful in areas where its teaching has been erroneous. Second, the vision commended by John Wilkins does not necessarily issue in the sentimentality associated with, say, John Lennon's 'Imagine'. Many of the features making modern life tolerant – and, indeed, tolerable – derive from secular thought. In important respects, Western society now casts the net of compassion more broadly than does the Catholic Church: one could cite, for example, a more grown-up attitude to homosexuals, divorcees, single parents and other former pariahs. (Some of the people interviewed for this book could remember a time when the names of alleged fornicators were read out from the pulpit Sunday by Sunday.) Nor is criticism of the Bishop of Rome necessarily a mark of disrespect. On the contrary, many Catholics argue that since he has unrivalled influence, and is the pre-eminent advocate of values without which the world will perish, it is essential to pitch the message credibly.

Third, although a church leader's style of government is likely to be informed by theological convictions, the two areas are logically distinct. A traditionalist, for instance, might share Benedict's doctrines, yet still judge that his bid to rein in dissent has been high-handed on occasion, and that the Congregation for the Doctrine of the Faith (CDF) sometimes displays a ruthlessness reminiscent of a secular dictatorship. The Pope's supporters deny this vehemently, and I have sought to give due weight to the case for the defence. But the critics include people of substance. Among them is Fr Henry Wansbrough, a British scholar who worked with Ratzinger on the Pontifical Biblical Commission. 'I don't know how someone so polite, so perceptive, so open, so intelligent, could also have put his name to so many severe pronouncements,' he told me.

The fourth ground some observers have for querying the Pope's platform is the most intriguing, because of its impeccable source, namely Benedict himself. He has not only changed over time. Even as the Church's chief doctrinal watchdog, he sometimes showed a wholly different private face. One of his fiercest statements, issued in 1989, warned Catholics against yoga and Eastern meditation practices. (Observers claim that he once described Buddhism as 'spiritual auto-eroticism', though the remark may have been misinterpreted.) But it is still little known outside academic circles that, in 1992, Ratzinger donated a large sum from his personal resources to finance a translation of the *Lotus Sutra* into German. The sentiment behind this generous act was underscored when he told an interviewer that Hermann Hesse's Buddhist-inspired novel *Siddhartha* was one of his three most treasured books, after the Bible and Augustine's *Confessions*, and that there are as many paths to God as there are human beings.[7]

Part of this reflects dialectics essential in any attempt, Christian or otherwise, to encompass the ineffable in language. Even the New Testament does not speak with one voice on the status of those outside the visible Church. No individual can have the last word on the relation between nature and grace, or on many other theological topics. Nevertheless, such vignettes point to an interesting dichotomy within Pope Benedict himself. The puzzle presented by this complex, talented man is real as well as apparent.

1

Boyhood

Joseph Ratzinger has always seen a good omen in his date of birth, 16 April 1927, because it was Holy Saturday, or Easter Eve. This interval after the Passion is associated both with a great settling of spiritual accounts (the Middle Ages, especially, saw a proliferation of stories about Christ's descent into hell to defeat the powers of evil), and with rejoicing: Joseph was baptised immediately, the priest using water newly blessed for the Easter vigil. The more he thought about it, Ratzinger later wrote, the more he saw a correspondence between Holy Saturday and Christian life generally. 'We are still awaiting Easter; we are not yet standing in the full light but walking toward it full of trust.'[1]

The political portents were clearly anything but good. Nazi demagogues had fed off Germany's chronic economic woes for much of the decade, and profited further from the Wall Street crash in 1929. But early signs of the horror that would almost overwhelm Europe were hard to trace in Joseph's first home, Marktl am Inn, a village 60 miles east of Munich. Standing inside a triangle formed on two sides by the Inn and Salzach rivers, Marktl in its daily life matched a template common to pre-industrial Catholic societies. Its rhythms were governed by the seasons and the church calendar.

Bavaria overall was less homogeneous. As the historian and biographer Nicholas Boyle has noted,[2] even as late as the Weimar era the old structure of the Holy Roman Empire could be traced in many of Germany's regions. It was still a country in which a patchwork of states, 'free cities and sovereign principalities, enclaves and exclaves, Catholics, Lutherans, and Calvinists, coexisted and proudly maintained their local independence, rights, and privileges'. Ratzinger has often referred approvingly to the part played by Catholics in resisting successive drives towards cultural uniformity, above all during Napoleonic times and Bismarck's Kulturkampf. 'Should Pope Benedict surprise us with a rediscovery of the Second Vatican Council's concern for collegiality and subsidiarity,' Boyle continues, 'he will have the resources of a long German tradition to call on.'[3]

Ratzinger begins *Milestones*, a brief memoir about the first five decades of his life, by tracing Bavaria's assorted Christian roots as far back as antiquity. There follows a sketch of his circumstances. He was the youngest of three like-minded siblings. His brother Georg (b 1924) was also to become a priest, and his sister Maria (b 1921) would live with Joseph for many years as his housekeeper until her death in 1991. Their parents, Maria and Joseph Sr, a policeman, were an intensely pious couple of modest means. In the best-known family photograph taken in the 1930s, Joseph and his father (on the left and right side of the frame respectively) are seated in half-profile, eyes averted from the camera. The only physical contact is between father and daughter: young Maria's forearm rests on Joseph Sr's shoulder. The impression given by this tableau reflects the Ratzingers' milieu in actuality: serious, respectable, rather rigid.

In 1929, they all moved to Tittmoning on the border with Austria, a town Ratzinger describes as 'my childhood's land of dreams'. Built in the Salzburg style, it is dominated by a fortress, and includes a large Baroque monastic church. The family's accommodation was directly above the police station, housed in the main building on the town square. These quarters were outwardly imposing, but poorly appointed on closer inspection. Yet the future Pope acknowledges his good fortune compared with many of his neighbours'. The beautiful façades of the town's houses belied the hardship suffered by many of their occupants; and with want came a susceptibility to extremist propaganda. By contrast, the surrounding countryside was a source of unmixed pleasure. The three children often walked to the top of the hill overlooking the Salzach, and visited a shrine in the woods, the Ponlach chapel. Crossing the river in Tittmoning brought them straight into Austria; this gave Joseph the frisson of being abroad, but the reassurance of remaining among people who spoke the same language, and almost the same dialect.

Ratzinger describes his father as an avowed anti-fascist whose position was threatened by his hostility to the Brownshirts. Within three years the family therefore moved again, this time to Aschau am Inn, a well-heeled village 20 miles closer to Munich. Their billet was a comfortable flat in a building attached to a meadow; nearby was a carp pond in which Joseph once almost drowned. Though missing the grandeur of Tittmoning, and noting the 'coarser' accents of their neighbours, the Ratzingers took a full part in parish life.

It was in the classroom that Joseph first felt the effects of National Socialism. The Catholic Church was Germany's largest single institution, with an unmatched social outreach through its network of schools, clubs, fellowships and publications. For much of the 1920s and early 1930s it had put up concerted resistance to the Nazis, especially through the Centre Party, a bastion of democratic moderation led by Monsignor Ludwig Haas. All this changed after Hitler became Chancellor on 30 January 1933. Within five months, he had signed a concordat with the Church negotiated by Cardinal Eugenio Pacelli, the future Pius XII, which purported to grant Catholic schools and clergy generous privileges. In return, the Vatican undertook to disband the Centre Party, and end formal church involvement in politics, as it had done in Italy through the 1929 Lateran Treaty.

Drawn up in secret over the heads of the German bishops, the concordat with Hitler has attracted a torrent of criticism in retrospect. Pacelli was partly motivated by a justified fear of Communism, which was shared by a large number of Catholics. To many Germans, Hitler's anti-Stalinist credentials constituted a virtue that outweighed his vices. But Pacelli's fundamental consideration was ecclesiological. The papacy's domination of church life, including all episcopal appointments, is a recent development dating from provisions in the revised Code of Canon Law of 1917. Before the twentieth century, the claim that popes are absolute monarchs was more a matter of theory than practice: its implementation was made possible only by the spread of modern communications. Germany had a long tradition of electing some of its bishops, and Pacelli was no enthusiast for dispersed power. To achieve his authoritarian vision of church government, he was ready to be indulgent towards political dictatorships.[4]

Looking back, Ratzinger grants that this stance was naïve at best. He writes movingly of how the world around him became steadily poisoned by Nazism, as Germany's new rulers quickly reneged on their promises to the Church. After the passing on 23 March 1933 of the Enabling Act, which gave Hitler power to rule Germany by decree, supporters of the far Right could declare open allegiance to a creed they had hitherto endorsed in private. A portion of Aschau's residents now began sporting Nazi regalia; Georg Ratzinger was press-ganged into the Hitler Youth, and his sister into a related body, the League of German Girls. (It is perhaps salutary for foreigners to be reminded that German civilians were among those hardest hit by the Third Reich, and that children were among Hitler's first victims.) Nazism proved seductive to various kinds of young people. A uniform put a working-class boy on the same level as the son of a professor. Independence from family and Church was encouraged, so National Socialism provided an effective channel for teenage rebellion. Members of the Hitler Youth were repeatedly told that they formed Germany's future, and that older people were a spent force. This, however, was anathema to the young Ratzingers, whose respect for their parents was unassailable.

The concordat included a stipulation that Catholic schools should retain their independent status, and catechesis remain in the hands of the clergy. But soon, in Ratzinger's words, his school's spiritual foundation 'was no longer to be the Christian faith but the ideology of the Führer'. *Milestones* suggests that a counter-attack by the country's bishops was heroic. Joseph was old enough to be deeply affected by the vehement tone of their pastoral letters. Yet despite his youth, it occurred to him that these messages 'in part misread the reality. I mean that merely to guarantee institutions is useless if there are no people to support those institutions from inner conviction . . . So . . . it was inane to insist on an institutionally guaranteed Christianity.'[5]

What did these developments imply? The moral and intellectual authority of the Catholic Church was certainly boosted to some extent after the Second World War, by dint of its numerical superiority in what became West Germany, and because it could appeal to a record of partial resistance to Hitler. As Nicholas Boyle argues in the article already cited, during a process of secularisation lasting more than 150 years, Germany's bureaucrats had by the 1930s moved away from their original Protestant faith into 'idealism, cultural nationalism, and, ultimately, nihilistic worship of the state'. The exclusion of Catholics from this process is now seen to have been a blessing, as many always believed.

In the long run, though, and despite his indirect criticism of Pacelli, Ratzinger has also drawn a conservative ecclesiological inference from the tragedy of 1933–45. Like John Paul II, whose papacy was informed by a sense that Polish Catholics could not have triumphed against Communist tyranny had they been permitted the luxury of dissent, Ratzinger has repeatedly argued that the Church is most effective when run as a tight ship. In the German context, however, the opposite conclusion is equally plausible: that Pacelli's policies unwittingly weakened the only force in Germany capable of thwarting Hitler, and that German Catholics were hamstrung throughout the 1930s by a tradition of docile obedience to authority.

This interpretation is strengthened by a less personal survey of the Church's record than Ratzinger supplies in *Milestones*. He rightly salutes the heroism of individuals, and his line of argument could be elaborated. Bishop Clemens von Galen of Münster's opposition to the Nazis came to a climax in 1941, when he preached a series of sermons condemning the Gestapo, concentration camps, euthanasia and forced sterilisation. He risked the death penalty for his pains. In Dachau, the large number of clerical inmates led to their being housed together in one building. Institutionally, the Catholic Church never endorsed Hitler as the Lutherans did through the Glaubensbewegung Deutsche Christen; and Pius XI condemned Nazism unequivocally in his encyclical *Mit brennender Sorge* ('With Burning Concern'), published in 1938. It is the only such document ever written in German, and had to be circulated secretly before being broadcast in sermons across the land.

But the broader picture is more mixed, and Ratzinger gives no hint of how Nazi rule was at times cemented by the collusion of Catholics. The Enabling Act itself was sealed only on the casting vote of Mgr Haas. Four days later, on 28 March, the German bishops rescinded the ban on Nazi party leadership that had been in force since August 1932, and after 1935, most Catholic clergy cooperated in implementing the Nuremberg laws forbidding marriage between Aryans and non-Aryans.

The one-sidedness of *Milestones* comes across especially in the paean to Cardinal Michael von Faulhaber, Archbishop of Munich, a man Ratzinger admired deeply. As a seminarian after the war, he observed that 'you could practically touch the burden of sufferings [Faulhaber] had had to bear during the Nazi period, which now enveloped him with an aura of dignity.' The Cardinal did indeed display great courage at times, and his residence was daubed with the slogan 'After the Jew, the Jew-lover.' Yet he had earlier praised the Führer for creating a new spirit of community, or *Volksgemeinschaft*, in Germany. Nor does Ratzinger reckon with a deeper problem, namely that many clergy of both main traditions found it very hard to condemn anti-Semitism outright, because of the Churches' manifest role in nourishing hostility to the Jews over many centuries.

Milestones condemns the effects of Nazi rule many times (and especially its effect on Catholics), but some readers have expressed surprise at the paucity of references to Hitler's Jewish victims. It could be argued in Ratzinger's defence that he is writing autobiographically, through the eyes of a boy. The book does not purport to be a history of Nazi Germany. But in the event, the Final Solution was to impinge on Joseph's experience briefly after the fall of Hungary in 1944, when he saw groups of Jews being transported to Auschwitz. He revealed this in an interview published in *Time* magazine (6 December 1993). *Milestones* does not mention it.

What the book reveals above all is the strength of Joseph's faith. It seemed to be confirmed rather than challenged by adversity. Nor is there any impression that he struggled over his vocation: religion ministered to his imagination and emotions, as well as to his intellect, and he took for granted that the priesthood would be his path. In 1935, Georg entered the *Gymnasium* at Traunstein, ten miles south of Tittmoning, and then transferred to the junior seminary in the same town. Joseph followed him. He modestly says that he could not compete with his elder brother in zeal, but his piety was evidently matched by high intelligence. A sense of his talents (and a premonition of liberal instincts) emerges in his enthusiasm for the *Schott*, a volume of liturgical texts with substantial chunks of parallel translation in German. Joseph says that his parents had been given a copy on their wedding day by 'a progressive pastor'. Their younger son later received an abridged and illustrated *Schott* for children, then a full version, and finally a complete Missal covering every day of the year. He expresses the intense attraction he felt towards Catholicism as follows:

Every new step into the liturgy was a great event for me. Each book I was given was something precious to me, and I could not dream of anything more beautiful. It was a riveting adventure to move by degrees into the mysterious world of the liturgy, which was being enacted before us and for us on the altar. It was becoming more and more clear to me that here I was encountering a reality that no one had simply thought up, a reality that no official authority or great individual had created. This mysterious fabric of texts and actions had grown from the faith of the Church over the centuries. It bore the whole weight of history within itself, and yet, at the same time, it was much more than the product of human history.[6]

As a policeman, Joseph Sr was obliged to retire from the force on his sixtieth birthday, in March 1937. Several years earlier he had bought an old farmhouse in Hufschlag, a hamlet on the edge of Traunstein. The property was served by its own well, and bounded on one side by oak trees and on the other by pine forest. (Today it retains its charm, despite standing beside a cluster of modern chalets, and is home to a donkey and a family of rabbits.) Moving there gave Joseph further opportunities to roam in beautiful surroundings. The bedroom he shared with Georg had picture-book views of two well-known local mountains, the Hochfellen and the Hochgern. Once enrolled at the *Gymnasium*, Joseph specialised in the classics. The teaching was a good deal more rigorous than at Aschau, and Ratzinger speaks of his lifelong gratitude for being made to master large portions of Latin. None of his teachers belonged to the Nazi party, but the headmaster was quickly ousted for failing to toe the new ideological line.

As John Allen, Ratzinger's first English-language biographer, has noted,[7] he is also surprisingly coy about acknowledging the extent of anti-Nazi activity on his doorstep. Among the brave spirits of Traunstein were Valentin Hasslberger who, as a Jehovah's Witness, refused to join the Wehrmacht; Rupert Berger, head of the local branch of the Bavarian People's Party, which had emerged from the Centre Party; and various figures associated with the White Rose, a fellowship dedicated to anti-Nazi subversion. There was also Fr Josef Stelzle, a Traunstein priest who condemned anti-Semitism in his homilies; and the anti-Nazi witness of assorted Communists. Ratzinger does not refer to any of these people in *Milestones*, even though Berger's son was his contemporary at seminary, and ordained alongside him. But several acts of small-scale defiance are recorded nonetheless.

Joseph and his classmates were supposed to sing Nazi slogans set to the tunes of old songs, but their teacher, a devout Catholic, encouraged them to replace phrases such as *'Judah den Tod'* ('Death to Judah') with *'Wende die Not'* ('Ease our plight').

In the mid-30s, the regime abolished the distinction between the humanities-based *Gymnasium* and the science-based *Realschule*, and introduced in its place a comprehensive *Oberschule* with a curriculum more focused on science and modern languages. Since Joseph was already established in the old system, he and his classmates were given leave to continue. A bigger change to his routine occurred at Easter 1939, when he entered junior seminary, with the blessing of his parish priest. The move entailed financial sacrifice for his parents, eased by help from his sister. Having passed her school exams, Maria had begun a clerical job in Traunstein.

The new recruit's hopes of happiness in a godly refuge were disappointed. Boarding school life was not to his taste, accustomed as he was to 'solitary ways', and he describes the experience of sitting in a study hall with 60 other boys as 'torture'. One of his later colleagues has gone further, telling me that Joseph 'had no friends at all' as a child, and was close only to his family. Sport was a particularly unpleasant ordeal for the slender, bookish boy, especially as he was the youngest of his intake: 'I must say that my fellow students were very tolerant of me, but in the long run it is not very pleasant to have to live on others' tolerance, knowing that you are nothing but a burden for the team to which you are assigned.'[8]

Ratzinger gives a powerful sense of how worried moderate Germans were by the slide towards war, and of their misgivings about appeasement. It was clear to the 11-year-old pupil, as well as to his parents, that Germany's seizure of the Sudetenland in 1938 was 'a postponement of, not a solution to, the problem'. Czechoslovakia was invaded in March 1939; six months later Poland was flattened by the now united forces of Hitler and Stalin. With the outbreak of full-scale conflict, Traunstein's junior seminary became a military hospital, and Joseph and his classmates were moved to premises owned by a local convent. That he took refuge in books for most of this time is scarcely surprising. He continued to steep himself in Latin and Greek literature, and ingested large doses of Goethe, and nineteenth-century writers such as Eichendorff, Mörike and Stifter.

He acknowledges that Germany's initially unstoppable advance was a source of patriotic pride, even to many opponents of Nazism. But *Milestones* absolves Joseph Sr of such short-sightedness: 'My father . . . was one who with unfailing clairvoyance saw that a victory of Hitler's would not be a victory for Germany but rather a victory of the Antichrist that would surely usher in apocalyptic times for all believers, and not only for them.'[9] By the time Hitler broke his accord with Stalin and invaded the Soviet Union in 1941, Joseph was maturing into a sharp observer of the international scene. That the Wehrmacht had overreached itself was confirmed in the schoolboy's mind by the lesson of Napoleon's assault on Russia. The turn of the tide was keenly felt in Traunstein: a growing number of public buildings were converted into military hospitals, as convoys brought back many severely mutilated soldiers, and the Ratzinger brothers returned to their parents. Georg, then 17, was called up in the autumn of 1942, and wounded in Italy two years later.

Germany's languishing fortunes brought inevitable demands for fresh military recruits, which had grievous consequences for many teenagers during the last two years of the war. From mid-1943, boarding school pupils around the country were sent to live in anti-aircraft units, or Flaks, and Joseph was assigned to one at Munich. The conscripts wore uniforms similar to those of regular soldiers, and helped to operate the artillery. At the same time they continued their studies, now at one of the city's famous schools, the Maximilians-Gymnasium. This was the junior seminarian's first experience of a more cosmopolitan environment. Like many able children raised a long way from the bright lights, he and his Traunstein contemporaries surpassed their Munich peers academically, but lacked their broader savoir-faire.

Joseph's tour of duty included stints at Ludwigsfeld, north of the city, protecting a BMW factory that was making aeroplane motors, and at Innsbruck in Austria. Sometimes he benefited from the kindness of strangers. At Gilching, west of Munich, for example, the boys were exempted from military exercises by a friendly non-commissioned officer, and Joseph was even assigned his own room. There were also regular opportunities for fellowship among the Catholic contingent, and times for private reading during spells of inaction.

Beyond the barracks lay a world half-ruined, of course. The boys' trips to Munich now grew more sporadic, as the city endured its first full aerial assault. But the gloom Joseph felt was alleviated by news of the Normandy landings. 'There was great trust in the Western powers and a hope that their sense of justice would also help Germany to begin a new and peaceful existence. However . . . none of us could be sure that he would live to return home from this inferno.'[10] Having reached military age, he was issued with the *Reichsarbeitsdienst*, a summons to serve the state, in early September of 1944. By the end of the month, he had moved to a barracks on the border between Austria, Hungary and Czechoslovakia commanded by older Nazis, some of whom had been among Hitler's earliest followers. Ratzinger represents them as unwavering fanatics. Their brief partly involved drill command and the supervision of trench-digging, but included a more sinister aspect: the recruiting of so-called volunteers for the SS. Joseph's announcement that he wished to become a priest drew a scornful reaction from these men, but it helped keep him in the ordinary ranks.

By October, Hungary had capitulated before the Soviet advance, and the preparation of anti-tank blockades in Joseph's company grew more frenetic. Surprisingly, their expectation of being drafted as regular soldiers did not materialise. Instead, in late November, they were given leave to return to their homes, a journey that took the Traunstein contingent through Vienna and Salzburg, previously pristine cities, now showing signs of heavy war damage. (Though not mentioning the Hungarian Jews, Ratzinger expresses particular anguish over the damage to Salzburg's Renaissance cathedral.) After three weeks with his parents Joseph was finally drafted into military service, and moved to Traunstein, where his superiors behaved more humanely. Many had experienced the hellish conditions of the Eastern front, and had no appetite for further conflict. Joseph was let off military drill because of an infected finger, and instead joined a group charged with boosting morale by marching round the town singing patriotic songs.

The futility of such displays was underwritten by Hitler's suicide on 30 April. Within days of learning this news, Joseph showed considerable independence of mind by breaking away from his companions and setting off for home. His action was hazardous, even though he stuck to country back routes, because deserters were often shot on sight. At one point, walking out of a railway underpass, he was intercepted by two soldiers, and feared for his life. Seeing the fugitive's arm in a sling, they decided to wave him on.

The return home was tinged with anxiety about the danger to which he was thereby exposing his parents, especially when two SS men arrived seeking shelter. They enquired about Joseph's circumstances, and then listened as his father denounced Hitler. In the event, the family suffered no reprisals on either score. *Milestones* describes the episode in characteristically reverent tones: 'a special angel seemed to be guarding us, and the two disappeared the next day without having caused any mischief.'[11]

When Joseph emerged from the house with raised hands 48 hours days later, he was confronted with the barrel of an American gun. Captured prisoners were marched for three days in constantly growing columns along an empty highway towards Bad Aibling, a rural town south of Munich. From there, Joseph's group was moved to farmland near the city of Ulm, on the border between Bavaria and Baden-Württemberg, where 50,000 Germans were corralled for several weeks in the open air. The daily ration was a ladle of soup and a small piece of bread. With his hopes of quick release dashed, the seminarian drew solace from taking part in sporadic worship organised by fellow prisoners, recording his thoughts in a notebook, and trying his hand at Greek hexameters.

The release of internees began in early June; Joseph emerged from behind the wire on the 19th. An American truck brought him as far as Munich, from where released prisoners were supposed to find their own ways home. He managed to hitch-hike most of the way. '[T]he heavenly Jerusalem itself could not have appeared more beautiful to me,' he declares of his arrival home before sunset. It was the feast of the Sacred Heart. His mother and sister were in church when Joseph walked into the village, but they hurried home afterwards to celebrate. Georg, who was not yet with them, returned from Italy in July. For Joseph, as for many young people, the remainder of 1945 was marked by elation at freedom regained, grief at the loss of so many contemporaries, and a fervent effort to join the dots of their former lives.

2

Studies

The brothers were destined for the major seminary at Freising, ancient heart of the Munich diocese, for the two years' philosophical study that formed the first phase of priestly formation. Their new home had lately served as a hospital for foreign POWs, and so the 120-strong body of first-year students lived in temporary accommodation for their first few terms. At 19, Ratzinger was among the youngest in this company, some members of which were twice his age. Many of the battle-scarred older candidates were sceptical about whether teenagers could possess the requisite fibre for ministry, but their mistrust was steadily allayed, partly by a recognition across the age groups that they were lucky to be alive at all.

They were also fortunate in their teachers. Ratzinger records a debt of gratitude to Jakob Fellermeier, who taught him ancient philosophy, and the rector, Michael Höck, who had spent five years in Dachau. Books were easier to come by in Freising than elsewhere; and the contents of the seminary library, mostly unscathed by the war, helped slake a general thirst for knowledge among the students. Their tastes were evidently eclectic. Popular choices included the novels of Ernst Wiechert, Gertrud von Le Fort and Elisabeth Langgässer; among foreign writers Dostoevsky, Bernanos and Claudel were particular favourites.

Like Hans Urs von Balthasar, Henri de Lubac and Romano Guardini, probably the three twentieth-century theologians he most admires, Ratzinger showed a strong preference for Augustine over Thomas Aquinas. In this respect, as we have seen, there was no shift in his view over time. The student found in Augustine's *Confessions* a psychological depth lacking in the 'impersonal', 'crystal-clear logic' of Aquinas, and other theologians whose thought he regarded as untutored by the heart. The cause of this reaction was in part presentational. For long periods after Thomas produced the *Summa Theologiae*, including during the approach to Vatican II, his work was often taught through manuals. The study of the text itself is a fairly recent innovation. Another aspect was political. Aquinas had been designated the Catholic Doctor par excellence by Pope Leo XIII at the end of the nineteenth century, and this gave his oeuvre a sacrosanct status that did not sit well with free enquiry. Ratzinger had an able teacher named Arnold Wilmsen who was acquainted with the main schools of modern Western philosophy. But Wilmsen's approach did not satisfy his abler students. Having also absorbed chunks of Heidegger, Husserl, Buber, all of whom were striving to revive questions about the meaning of life after Kant's assault on the noumenal (that is, allegedly unknowable) realm, Ratzinger could not rest content with pat answers.

Augustine has broad appeal. For all the political turbulence around him, he lived in a world where philosophers and theologians could draw on an integrated intellectual heritage focused on reality and the search for truth. He took for granted a reciprocally enabling connection between reason and faith. Reading the *Confessions*, Ratzinger found a correlation between the message of the gospel and the truth uncovered in the arts and other spheres of study. This intuition rests on a yet more basic conviction common to many strands of Christian thought. Ratzinger skates over the subject in *Milestones*, but it perhaps needs spelling out. To the atheist's challenge that Christian teaching, especially about the resurrection, goes beyond the evidence of history or experience, the believer can reply: Why is there something rather than nothing? Science accounts for a potentially infinite causal chain, but it cannot explain the existence of the universe as such. And while it may not be unreasonable to have doubts about the resurrection, it *is* unreasonable to doubt the reality of the world around us; yet the latter is arguably an even greater miracle. The belief that we are created – and destined for communion with the source of our being – is thus a warranted conclusion of metaphysical reasoning. From this springs Ratzinger's characteristically Augustinian conviction that it isn't reasonable to think that only reason discloses the world. The texture of reality is revealed by reason combined with our ethical and aesthetic impulses.

Augustine's God is active in making himself known to humanity in concrete terms, and Ratzinger's writings, especially on pastoral matters, are steeped in this tradition. It seems to have nourished his gift for the telling phrase. In *Der Gott Jesu Christi*, for example, a little book based on addresses during the 1970s, he says that while the biblical God has a name and gives names to others, the Antichrist in the Book of Revelation is a number. Ratzinger then tells his audience that they have all lived through an age when people were known by their numbers in extermination camps, so they know how the Antichrist works.

Milestones also reports the excitement the seminarians felt at the changes of world view brought in by quantum physics, and the discovery that the physical world is not a closed system. Since classical materialism was now being undermined by science itself, they reasoned, then religion (including the belief that matter is a reflection of a deeper, veiled reality) need not involve the special pleading associated with the God of the gaps. What Ratzinger does not mention is that he was an unusually bright boy – and an accomplished amateur pianist – with broader horizons than might be expected from someone of his background. In 1947, he moved to the Herzogliches Georgianum, a residence for theological students attached to the University of Munich. His memoir bashfully represents this as a matter of personal choice; in reality he could not have left Freising without his Archbishop's say-so. Reports of the young man's gifts had reached senior figures in the diocese, and only two other students moved to Munich with him.

The university was still largely a ruin, and at this time seminarians had to be accommodated in the small castle at Fürstenried, south of Munich, which had once served as a royal hunting lodge. They were housed in a cramped annex to the main building, and slept in bunk beds. Some of their lectures were given in a greenhouse. Again, though, nature offered a refuge from material hardship. The grounds contained French- and English-style gardens in which Ratzinger roamed frequently. He sometimes returned to Fürstenried throughout the decades until becoming Pope, finding that a stroll down the gravel drives always released a flock of blithe memories.

Milestones tells much about the shaping of a potent – if sometimes fitful – theological voice. In the first place, we are told that scholars (biblical commentators especially) had in the recent past faced heavy Vatican sanctions for the crime of intellectual honesty, and that Ratzinger shared the liberal indignation at such treatment. Action of this kind would not recede until after Vatican II, but the Cardinal confines his criticism to the pre-First World War era, which was even harsher. The local cause célèbre was Friedrich Wilhelm Maier, who taught New Testament studies at Fürstenried. Before 1914, he had come to accept a hypothesis about the ordering of the Synoptic Gospels pioneered by nineteenth-century Protestants, and later almost universally accepted by exegetes. Known as the two-source theory, this holds that Mark wrote first, and that Matthew and Luke then composed their Gospels independently of one another, using Mark and a conjectural document that does not survive called Q (from the German for source, *Quelle*) as their main raw materials. The Catholic Church in the early twentieth century refused to countenance any challenge to traditional belief in the priority of Matthew. As a young scholar Maier was deprived of his chair, and became an army chaplain until his rehabilitation during the 1920s. An obvious implication of this apparently technical dispute is that a Vatican clampdown can sometimes look foolish as well as severe. In biblical studies as in other departments, the Catholic Church has ended up stealing the clothes of those it once condemned.

Ratzinger gives an even-handed summary of Maier's strengths:

> From a distance of nearly fifty years, I can once again see what was truly positive there: the candid questions from the perspectives of the liberal-historical method created a new directness in the approach to Sacred Scripture and opened up dimensions of the text that were no longer perceived by the all-too-predetermined dogmatic reading. The Bible spoke to us with new immediacy and freshness.[1]

He also concedes that 'many a Roman decision' drew a scornful response from him and others, and a sense that they in Germany knew better than 'those down there' in the Vatican.

Then *Milestones* changes gear. In a brief passage foreshadowing his much-discussed pronouncements on the ecclesial vocation of the theologian, Ratzinger says that 'such reservations and sentiments did not for a moment diminish the deep assent of our faith to the primacy in the form in which the First Vatican Council defined it.' He illustrates his point with reference to a debate on

Mary's Assumption involving another of his teachers, Gottlieb Söhngen. The doctrine was defined *ex cathedra* by Pius XII in 1950, having been generally believed, but not as a dogma, by Catholics for many centuries. It forms a substantial ecumenical stumbling block for many theologians and others in the Reformed traditions, who point out that the belief is found earliest in a third-century heretical text. What is more, by pronouncing definitively on what had until then strictly speaking been a matter of opinion, Pius was adding to the deposit of faith. Belief in the Virgin's bodily Assumption was now to be regarded by Catholics as necessary to salvation.

For these and other reasons, Söhngen 'held forth passionately against the possibility of this Marian dogma' during a debate with Protestants in 1949. He was then asked whether he wouldn't have to leave the Church if the belief were formally spelt out. Ratzinger quotes his reply with approval: 'If the dogma comes, then I will remember that the Church is wiser than I and that I must trust her more than my own erudition.'[2]

A hostile verdict on Ratzinger's change of perspective would see it as an instance of liberalism betrayed. For his defenders, this is to overlook the subtlety of his argument, and the premise underlying it: that Catholics cannot afford the luxury of sectarianism, because they form part of a conversation linking continents and cultures, and reaching backwards and forwards in time. The Assumption is an unusual case because it is the only article of belief ever to have prompted an infallible statement, apart from the claim to infallibility itself. On other matters, the line separating private judgement and the collective mind of the Church is less stable. The question of how this line should be policed has underlain almost every major dispute of Ratzinger's career.

If he were asked now to speak in his own defence, Pope Benedict's argument might run as follows. Roman Catholicism must acknowledge a deep debt to Protestant standard-bearers in such fields as biblical studies, while remaining clear that Catholics have resources that equip them to avoid some of the pitfalls into which Reformed theologians have sometimes fallen. Debate over the incarnation forms a prominent example of this. When nineteenth- and early twentieth-century scholars first suggested that the doctrine derived more from contamination by Platonist influences during the second and third centuries than from the New Testament itself, the idea sent shockwaves through the

Protestant world. Catholics were far less agitated, because of their organic understanding of the relation between Scripture and tradition. They would add that the New Testament, though definitive, is a work in progress. If its edges are a bit rough in places, then this underscores the importance of tradition, an insight prefigured by Jesus' promise in John 16 that the Holy Spirit would lead the Church into all truth.

Exegesis, Ratzinger remarks in *Milestones*, 'has always remained for me the centre of my theological work'. Liturgy also takes pride of place among his concerns, and here, too, he expresses both liberal and conservative impulses which help account for his intellectual evolution. From Augustine, Bonaventure, von Balthasar and other theologians influenced by Platonism, he has always had a strong sense of the connection between beauty and truth. Good liturgy, then, far from being a matter of fussing about rubrics, entails a vital concern that the true and the beautiful somehow appear together. On this understanding, worshippers are involved in the life of heaven, experiencing in a fragmentary way the world to come, and glimpsing God's purposes for the whole of creation.

Ratzinger's initial attitude towards the liturgical movement (a groundswell of opinion in the 1940s and 50s seeking reforms such as vernacular worship) was negative. Before reaching the Georgianum, he found in the reformers 'a one-sided rationalism and historicism that . . . exhibited a remarkable coldness when it came to dispositions of mind and heart that allow us to experience the Church as the place where the soul is at home'.[3] But he was won over by his lecturer on pastoral theology, Joseph Pascher. Under Pascher's tutelage, Ratzinger came to see liturgy as the 'living element' of theology, 'without which it would necessarily shrivel up'. It was on this ground that he welcomed the prospect of liturgical change at Vatican II, and advised his then Archbishop, Cardinal Joseph Frings, to approve the draft of the Constitution on the Liturgy, *Sacrosanctum Concilium*. Later, he revised his opinions drastically. 'I was not able to foresee that the negative sides of the liturgical movement would afterward reemerge with redoubled strength, almost to the point of pushing the liturgy toward its own self-destruction.'[4]

By the autumn of 1949, reconstruction at the Georgianum was well enough advanced for students to return to Munich, though their material conditions remained bleak. Some thought that their quality of life would at least be enhanced by friendships with students in other faculties, but such contact did not materialise, given the proximity of final examinations the following year. With that hurdle cleared, the graduate was confronted with others almost at once. The pastoral part of his training, culminating in his ordination the following summer, still lay before him, and he also entered an extended-essay competition on the ecclesiology of St Augustine that was to form the basis of his doctorate. Now back in the seminary at Freising, he devoted much of his time to this project, while also receiving training in homiletics, catechesis and related subjects.

Finally, on the feast of SS Peter and Paul in 1951, Joseph, Georg and over forty other ordinands were ordained as priests in Freising's cathedral by Cardinal Faulhaber. It was the high point of Ratzinger's life before his election as Pope. A photo taken before the service shows a handsome, willowy young man in full pre-conciliar fig, looking expectant and a bit tense. 'We should not be superstitious,' he warns,

> but, at the moment when the elderly archbishop laid his hands on me, a little bird – perhaps a lark – flew up from the high altar in the cathedral and trilled a little joyful song. And I could not but see in this a reassurance from on high, as if I heard the words 'This is good, you are on the right way.'[5]

The following weeks felt like a non-stop feast to the Ratzinger brothers, reflecting the status enjoyed by many clerics in the 1950s. They were the toast of Traunstein, where they returned to celebrate their first Eucharists, and received invitations to bless innumerable people and their homes. A first-Mass card for each brother was reprinted in the local paper; Joseph's bore an inscription from 2 Corinthians 1:24: 'Not that we lord it over your faith; we work with you for your joy, for you stand firm in your faith.' On 1 August, they began their lives as curates, Joseph having been assigned to the parish of the Precious Blood in the suburbs of Munich. Though well off for the most part, his congregation included a large minority of people in domestic service, and there were many balls to be kept in the air. The parish priest, a Fr Blumschein, did not spare himself, Ratzinger says, so nor did those around him. Still only 24, the new arrival had to celebrate and preach at two Masses each Sunday, and give

16 hours' religious instruction per week at five different levels. He heard confessions every weekday morning from 6 till 7 a.m., and for four hours on Saturday afternoons. There was also a constant round of baptisms, funerals, weddings and parish visiting.

He admits to having 'some difficulty' with these duties because of his 'scant practical training', but adds that they grew less onerous with time. Yet his experience of church life at the grassroots would remain limited. After serving for just 14 months, he was reassigned to full-time doctoral studies at Freising, and writes that he moved back with mixed feelings, having grown to enjoy life in the presbytery. In some ways, a year had been enough to knock the edges off him. Though he would later be described by critics as lacking common sense, Ratzinger acknowledges the difference between theory and practice that many of the newly ordained are obliged to surmount. 'To be sure, it also became evident how far removed the world of the life and thinking of many children was from the realities of faith and how little our religious instruction coincided with the actual lives and thinking of our families.'[6]

As we have seen, Ratzinger's interest in the Church Fathers was based on an urge to penetrate behind the thickets of scholasticism. His doctorate, though a less arduous qualification than in some other countries, was still taxing. It involved eight written papers, the same number of oral examinations, and an open debate. The thesis was passed in mid-1953. Like others aspiring to a full-scale academic career in Germany, he next had to write a post-doctoral thesis known as the *Habilitationsschrift*. Söhngen advised him to turn from the patristic period to the Middle Ages, and from ecclesiology to the doctrine of revelation. Ratzinger elected to concentrate on Bonaventure's understanding of salvation history (*Heilsgeschichte*) – the idea that revelation not only entails the communication of truth to the human intellect, but embraces a wider theatre. At the time, Protestants were putting their own gloss on this notion, but characteristically, Ratzinger's aim was to buttress a contemporary Catholic understanding.

He argues that in the high Middle Ages, revelation was generally thought of as denoting an act: 'the word refers to the act in which God shows himself, not the objectified result of this act.' In other words, the recipient is always part of the picture. This has important implications, one of which is that Scripture cannot itself be seen as revelation, but, rather, as a witness to revelation.

As the historian Lucy Beckett has remarked, 'the gap between the words, the languages of fallen humanity and the truth that is in God is never closed except in the Word that became flesh, and even then not in humanly told news of him.'[7] Barth and other Protestants also accepted this argument, but the Catholic corollary drawn by Ratzinger is that 'there can be no such thing as pure *sola Scriptura* ["by Scripture alone" – a Reformation shibboleth], because an essential element of Scripture is the Church as understanding subject, and with this the fundamental sense of tradition is already given.'[8]

Such material could be greatly elaborated at a scholarly level. The essential point for our purposes is that despite Ratzinger's willingness to fly the Catholic flag, and the fact that Bonaventure's arguments support conservative conclusions which help explain some of Ratzinger's later attitudes and policies, his work was considered risqué in what was still an extremely strict climate, and this put him on a collision course with some of his seniors. Four points in particular were liable to get him into trouble. First, his emphasis on the disposition of the recipient of revelation left him open to the charge of subjectivism; second, he was also running a risk through his considerable reliance on the latest French scholarship, viewed at the time with great suspicion in Rome and elsewhere. Third, there was his apparent impetuosity. 'With a forthrightness not advisable in a beginner,' Ratzinger confesses, he had not stinted in his criticism of several more established theologians. Finally, he was let down by a sloppy typist who taxed his nerves 'to the limit' by mixing up many of his references. He managed to correct some, but not all, of the errors.

The battle that ensued over Ratzinger's *Habilitation* would be the first of several in which he played David to the Goliaths of officialdom; and it almost laid waste to his career at a stroke. A sequence of unhappy events began in 1955, when a large house in Freising became available on the death of a former professor at the town's College, or *Hochschule*, for Philosophy and Theology. Ratzinger was pleased to accept an offer of the property, partly because it would provide a chance for his parents to move in with him. Now in their seventies, they had been finding it hard to live at a distance from their local amenities (Traunstein's main shops lay 2 km from Hufschlag).

They arrived towards the end of the year, by which time the *Habilitation* had been finished and read by Professor Söhngen, who approved it. The other reader, Professor Michael Schmaus, was apparently burdened with other work, and let the manuscript gather dust for two months before suddenly announcing at Easter that it did not pass muster. Ratzinger was horrified. He now had to reckon with a change of career, probably in a parish post, as well as the loss of the new family home, and says that the experience led him to side with the underdog in many later conflicts. Then came a chance of deliverance. A meeting of the theology faculty evidently saw a sharp exchange of views on the candidate's proficiency; Schmaus wielded more clout than Söhngen, but in the end they decided to return the thesis to Ratzinger for revision, rather than reject it outright.

Noticing that his chapter on Bonaventure's interpretation of history had drawn almost no hostile comment at all, he asked the examiners if they would settle for an expanded version of this section, and received a favourable reply. The chapter contained material on the prophecies of Joachim of Fiore, a twelfth-century Italian abbot who thought that history could be divided into three discrete phases; and that the third, known as the Kingdom of the Holy Spirit, and marked by love and liberty, was materialising during his own lifetime. (His ideas would indirectly influence later schools of historicist thought, including Marxism, Hegelianism and some forms of liberation theology.) *Milestones* contends that many other scholars doubted whether Bonaventure had ever engaged with Joachim, but Ratzinger was the first to discredit this assumption. He adds that Bonaventure was a man of the centre who recognised the need for 'ecclesial order'.

His *Habilitation* was resubmitted in October 1956, and after months of near-chronic anxiety he was notified of its acceptance on 11 February 1957. A public defence of the document – no mere formality – followed ten days later, and this was also judged satisfactory after further wrangles among the examiners. But Ratzinger's mood remained downbeat. 'I could hardly feel any joy, so heavily did the nightmare of what had happened weigh me down.'[9]

Even if the meteoric rise that followed was not predictable at this point, his prospects were pretty solid. He was briefly a lecturer, or *Privatdozent*, at the University of Munich, and in early 1958, 'not without some sniper shots from certain disgruntled quarters', he was appointed to a chair at the *Hochschule* in Freising. Though strained at first, his relations with Schmaus improved. Ratzinger continued to believe that his elder colleague's decision had been mistaken, but grants that the ordeal was 'healthy for me humanly speaking'. Within six months he was invited to become professor of fundamental (that is, philosophical) theology at Bonn, while Georg, who had been studying music in Munich, was at the same time appointed director of music in the family's old parish of St Oswald's, Traunstein. A house in the town centre came with the job, and although their parents had only recently uprooted themselves, the brothers calculated that Joseph Sr and Maria might be induced to return to the town they knew and loved.

Instead, an apparently serendipitous development became the source of a family rift. Joseph Sr was instinctively opposed to the idea, then gave way. But Ratzinger did not confide in his mother at first, thinking it might cause her needless anxiety in advance of a firm decision. When he and Georg broke the news, she had already heard about it from a third party. In *Milestones* we read that for some time afterwards Mrs Ratzinger 'suffered from what she perceived had been a lack of trust on [her sons'] part'.[10]

The Bonn phase of Ratzinger's career began in mid-April 1959, and proved highly congenial, as well as mind-broadening. Germany's cultural diversity meant that his translation several hundred miles to the north-west almost felt like a move to another country: the Rhineland had long been known as the gate to France. For a while he lived at a riverside residence for theological students called the Albertinum. It gave him views of the commercial fleets passing in and out of the area, which added to the sense of being at a crossroads. The Catholic presence was reasonably strong. Cities such as Cologne and Aachen lay nearby, and the new professor quickly made connections with the local outposts of the Dominicans, Franciscans and Divine Word Missionaries, among other orders.

There are usually separate Protestant and Catholic theological faculties in German universities, and Ratzinger does not appear to have had strong ecumenical contacts at this stage. His closest links were with historians such as Theodor Klauser and Hubert Jedin; Werner Schöllgen, a moral theologian, and two fellow doctrinal specialists, Johann Auer and Ludwig Hödl. The interdisciplinary friendships he struck tended to be with other Catholics, among them Paul Hacker, an erudite but volatile Indologist who had once been a Lutheran.

The sense of a fresh start in agreeable surroundings was

consolidated during his first term, when Ratzinger moved to a house in Bad Godesberg, just outside the city. A melancholy turn of events lay just ahead, however. In August, he returned with Maria to visit their parents in Traunstein. Joseph Sr had suffered a small stroke the previous summer, and had given the impression of believing that he was close to death from Christmas 1958 onwards. Eight months later, he collapsed on the steps of Georg's house at the end of a family supper, and died after 48 hours of intense pain. His children naturally felt relieved to be with him at the end, but were thereafter marked by a sense of dislocation. Ratzinger says little about his father, other than asserting that they were close. He felt hollowed out on returning to Bonn, as if a portion of his home 'had been transferred to the other world'.

Maria's widowhood did not last long. In early 1963, she showed symptoms of stomach cancer, and was reduced to skin and bones by the autumn. Having collapsed one day in November, she never left her sickbed, and died on 16 December. Ratzinger writes that the 'radiance of her goodness' has lived on, and that he knows of no more convincing proof for Christian belief than 'the pure and unalloyed humanity that the faith allowed to mature in my parents and in so many other persons I have had the privilege to encounter'.

The most important fillip in his early career came at this time. He hadn't got on well with Faulhaber's successor as Archbishop of Munich, but Ratzinger's relations with the Archbishop of Cologne, Cardinal Joseph Frings, were much better. The two were introduced by Hubert Luthe, Frings's secretary, who'd trained with Ratzinger at Fürstenried. They became friends, and the budding scholar was appointed Frings's *peritus*, or theological expert, at Vatican II. It gave him a ringside seat during the drama that was about to unfold.

3

Vatican II in Actuality
and Retrospect

When he convoked the Second Vatican Council, Pope John XXIII famously said that the Catholic faith, though unchanging in content, should be proclaimed to the contemporary world in a fresh way. His call was answered by the largest shake-up in church life for four centuries. Few would have predicted this, especially as curial hard-liners, at first opposed in principle to John's project, then sought to ensure that little or nothing new would come of it. The motto of Ratzinger's predecessor but two at the CDF (then called the Holy Office), Cardinal Alfredo Ottaviani, was *Semper idem*, 'Always the Same'. He and others thought that the gathering could be wrapped up in short order. Their strategy was to produce drafts (schemata) of council documents, and get them voted through briskly, with a minimum of debate. The most dramatic sign of imminent change came when the assembled bishops threw out the first of these texts, and moved to fix their imprint on all future proceedings.

Their *coup d'Église*, as it has been called, was reflected in *Lumen Gentium* ('Light of the World'), the Dogmatic Constitution on the Church. Its first chapter speaks of the irreducible diversity of models of the Church; but its second gives relative precedence to one image – that of the people of God. Nicholas Lash, among others, sees momentous change reflected in this move: 'It immediately means that you're not, as it were, starting at the top and moving downwards and outwards. We find all the Vatican I material repeated in Chapter 3 of *Lumen Gentium* – including the key features of teaching on the primacy – but they're now set in the context of the fact that the Catholic Church has an episcopal, collegial structure.'[1] Ratzinger was among those who saw *Lumen Gentium* as pivotal, and he contributed to its sections on collegiality.

As indicated, *Gaudium et Spes* deals with the Church in the contemporary world, and carries this more inclusive approach into the realm of anthropology. Catholics were no longer to be thought of as warriors in a citadel, but pilgrims walking alongside those who did not share their faith. Other conciliar documents evince a similar sea-change in attitudes. The Church that had previously denied the principle of freedom of conscience on the grounds that 'error has no rights' could now accept religious and other liberties. A hand of friendship was extended to what Paul VI – Giovanni Battista Montini, elected to succeed John in 1963 – would later call 'sister Churches'; and hopes for reunion were nourished on the basis of a common baptism.

Most striking for many laypeople, perhaps, was the reform of eucharistic and other rites set in train by *Sacrosanctum Concilium* (the main document on liturgy). Latin would give way to vernacular languages, partly because of the Church's revived sense of itself as a Communion of Communions. Each local Church could be seen more clearly as the whole Church in its own part of the world, and thus entitled to incarnate the faith in that cultural setting. During the liturgical upheaval which followed the Council, priests moved from an east-facing to a westward position at the altar, and many saw rich symbolism in this change: the people, having been the object of the action of the Mass, would now become the subject of it, as priest and people were seen to be united in the experience of the one Eucharist.

In some ways, Vatican II is a casualty of its own success. Its reforms have been so far-reaching that one can forget how different church life was until the mid-1960s. John Wilkins, an Anglican when the Council began, became a Roman Catholic under its impact. He was first struck by the plump, smiling and immensely likeable Pontiff who formed such a contrast with the other-wordly Pius XII: 'Here was a Pope like the fisherman Peter. You could almost see him casting out his nets, you could almost feel his love for the whole world.' On reflection, Wilkins saw the conduct of the Council as not only courageous, but self-authenticating:

I could see it came from a Christian community that felt itself to be connected in a special way with the Upper Room in

33

Jerusalem where the Church began. The Catholic Church, I suddenly saw, was attached to that Upper Room as by an umbilical cord that ran through the centuries up till now. And therefore it had a unique hold on the apostolic tradition, leading to a willingness to return to the sources in a trans- forming way . . . Before the council ended, I had become a Catholic.[2]

The 1960s was therefore a period of high hopes for the Church's more liberal wing. Yet the Council left some important loose ends. As we have seen, it enunciated the doctrine of episcopal collegiality: that church government is a matter for the bishops, '*cum et sub Petro*' (with and under the Pope), operating together as a college in succession to the apostles. At the same time, it restated earlier definitions of absolute papal primacy, and accepted moves by Paul VI to insert a so-called *nota praevia* into reports of conciliar proceedings. This was an official explanation of how the material on primacy and collegiality in Chapter 3 of *Lumen Gentium* was to be understood. It declared that 'as supreme pastor of the Church, the Sovereign Pontiff can always exercise his authority as he chooses, as is demanded by his office itself'; and was written to reassure those who thought that what the Council was saying about collegiality would compromise what Vatican I had declared about papal primacy. Ratzinger was so upset by Paul's intervention that at one point he urged the bishops to vote down the entire chapter. But the Pope got his way, insisting that the *nota* be included in all editions of *Lumen Gentium*.

So while there was a strong case for thinking that Paul had a moral obligation to operate collegially, he and his successors would retain the *de jure* right to rule as absolute monarchs. The best-known test case of the new climate arose in 1968, when the Pope ignored the majority view of his commission on birth control and reaffirmed the Church's ban on artificial contraception in his encyclical *Humanae Vitae*. Several bishops' conferences then declared family planning to be be a matter of conscience, but this was denied by Paul, and later (with growing vehemence) by John Paul II, who both believed that the centre might not hold in such circumstances. The illustration is important for understanding Ratzinger's trajectory. Though he was in favour of greater pluralism for much of the 1960s, his assessment would increasingly match that of the Roman authorities thereafter.

Anyone is naturally entitled to change his or her mind, even if, as in Ratzinger's case, the change was dramatic. As notable as his about-turn, however, is his reluctance to admit that it took place. For a clearer view of the record, we need to consider what *Milestones* does not tell us. One point to bear in mind (admittedly hard for Ratzinger himself to make without sounding immodest) is that his behind-the-scenes role at the Council was greater than that of almost any other *peritus*, for the simple reason that Cardinal Frings was a leader of the initial rebellion against the Curia, and a major player from then on. Officially, the *periti* were supposed to keep a low profile, and answer only questions specifically addressed to them. In practice, an able lieutenant was almost bound to stand out, especially one who shared the reformist instincts of his patron. And since Frings's eyesight was very poor, he was all the more reliant on Ratzinger, who would contribute to the documents on divine revelation, mission, and the Church in the modern world as well as on ecclesiology. A further considera-tion concerns the prestige and influence of the German-speaking bloc at the Council, and a widely shared sense that Germany, with France, provided the theological vanguard. (An early book about Vatican II was appropriately entitled *The Rhine Flows into the Tiber*.[3]) Helmut Krätzl, then a seminarian at the Anima, Rome's German-speaking college, and later an auxiliary bishop in the Vienna diocese, has written that Ratzinger '[exerted] himself energetically for a renewed vision of the Church' at this time, drawing plaudits from all quarters.

Before the Council's business began in earnest in October 1962, the bishops were asked to elect members of the commissions that would scrutinise conciliar texts in detail. Alarmed that their colleagues were being strong-armed into action before having a chance to get to know one another, Frings and the Bishop of Lille, Cardinal Achille Liénart, suggested a delay, so that more information on candidates could circulate first. Frings later described the official schema on divine revelation that had been proposed as 'inadequate', and Ratzinger shared his boss's view, calling the rejection of the drafts a 'genuinely positive' develop-ment. We know this because Ratzinger wrote short reflections after each conciliar session, and several commentaries on various aspects of the Council's work. The first of these, composed in 1966, says of the episode that there was a certain discomforting feeling that the whole enterprise might [amount] to nothing more than a mere rubber-stamping of the decisions already made, thus impeding rather than fostering the renewal needed in the Catholic Church. The Council would have disappointed and discouraged all those who had placed their hopes in it; it would have paralysed all their healthy dynamism and swept aside once again the many questions people of our era had put to the Church.[4]

With the rejection of the schema on revelation, attention in various quarters shifted to a draft text on the subject which Ratzinger had been writing alongside Karl Rahner (with whom, he says in *Milestones*, he had developed a 'very warm personal relationship' after their first meeting in 1956); this was debated at the Anima in late October in the presence of Montini, Liénart and Cardinal Léon Suenens, the influential Archbishop of Malines-Brussels. Rahner and Ratzinger's chief objection was to a model that conceived of revelation positivistically, as a box of facts. Their alternative proposals, much influenced by existentialism, were also found wanting, and there are few traces of their arguments in the final text, *Dei Verbum*, which was officially approved on 18 November 1965.

* * *

To many observers, the battle over a more consensual style of church government was crystallised by a famous showdown between Frings and Ottaviani in November 1963. Rumours spread that a vote in favour of greater collegiality a week beforehand had been queried by certain influential conservatives. Frings saw this as wrecking tactics. He reminded the commission that its primary duty was to serve the bishops, not the Vatican bureaucracy: 'The commission has no other function but to execute the wishes of . . . the Council.' Then Frings turned his fire on Ottaviani himself: 'This also goes for the Holy Office, whose methods and behaviour do not conform at all to the modern era, and are a cause of scandal to the world.' The broadening sweep of his complaints betokened years of pent-up frustration against a maximalist approach to intellectual uniformity: 'No one should be judged and condemned without being heard, without knowing what he is accused of, and without having the opportunity to amend what he can reasonably be reproached with.'

This drew a tigerish riposte from Ottaviani, who questioned the basis for collegiality (he once claimed that the only collegial act recorded in the Gospels was the disciples' flight from the Garden of Gethsemane), and insisted that the Holy Office's procedures were beyond reproach. But the tide of events appeared to be flowing Frings's way. His speech received lengthy applause, and a personal message of support from Pope Paul. It is highly likely that the author of Frings's speech was Ratzinger himself.

As Prefect of the CDF, he would develop a much cooler attitude towards episcopal conferences. His earlier, positive view of the subject is summed up in his article 'The pastoral implications of collegiality' for the inaugural issue of the journal *Concilium* in 1965:

> Let us dwell for a moment on the bishops' conferences, for these seem to offer themselves today as the best means of concrete plurality in unity. They have their prototype in the synodal activity of the regionally different 'colleges' of the ancient Church. They are also a legitimate form of the collegiate structure of the Church. One not infrequently hears the opinion that the bishops' conferences lack all theological basis and could therefore not act in a way that could be binding on an individual bishop. The concept of collegiality, so it is said, could be applied only to the common action of the entire episcopate. Here again we have a case where a one-sided and unhistorical systematisa-tion breaks down . . . We would rather say that the concept of collegiality, besides the office of unity which pertains to the pope, signifies an element of variety and adaptability that basically belongs to the structure of the Church, but may be actuated in many different ways. The collegiality of bishops signifies that there should be in the Church (under and in the unity guaranteed by the primacy) an ordered plurality. The bishops' conferences are, then, one of the possible forms of collegiality that is here partially realized but with a view to the totality.[5]

Turning to the account of Vatican II provided in Ratzinger's memoir, we find a very different picture. The tone is often defensive, with much being made of alleged misinterpretations of council documents. It confirms the impression that in some ways

Milestones tells us more about the Cardinal during the 1990s than the putative object of his study. Any sense that revolution was in the air is given short shrift. For many, Ratzinger writes, the prospect of a general Council 'reanimated and . . . intensified even to the point of euphoria the atmosphere of renewal and hope that had reigned in the Church and in theology since the end of the First World War despite the perils of the National Socialist era'.[6] This statement, while not wrong, is not right either, as a glance at Ratzinger's own comments – including in earlier passages of *Milestones* already quoted – demonstrates. And it does scant justice to the dozens of theologians whose work was vindicated at Vatican II after years of harassment by the Holy Office beforehand.

Of the draft texts forwarded to him by Frings, Ratzinger writes that he naturally 'took exception to certain things', but 'found no grounds for a radical rejection of what was being proposed, such as many demanded later on in the Council and actually managed to put through'. He acknowledges that the documents 'bore only weak traces' of the biblical and patristic renewal pioneered by devotees of *ressourcement* during the 1930s, 40s and 50s, 'so that they gave an impression of rigidity and narrowness through their excessive dependence on scholastic theology'. But Ratzinger treats these with deference nevertheless, saying that they had a 'solid' basis.

He then elaborates his understanding of revelation, which closely matches a central argument of his *Habilitation*, and contrasts this with what he sees as the prevailing model, much influenced by a Tübingen theologian, J. R. Geiselmann. In a long technical digression, *Milestones* represents Geiselmann as arguing (partly on the basis of a reinterpretation of documents from the Council of Trent) that both Scripture and tradition contain the whole of revelation, and therefore, in effect, that biblical commentators should be free to elaborate their theories independently of church control – and indeed to instruct church leaders, rather than to learn from them. Ratzinger dismisses what he alleges to be Geiselmann's theory for predictable reasons: revelation requires a recipient; so Scripture cannot be unshackled from tradition in the manner envisaged by Protestantism. Loosening the cords that bind them leads to all manner of error.

Both the form and content of this argument are surprising. First, the preparatory theological commission's rejected draft on revelation was also defective from Ratzinger's point of view. Its very title – *De Fontibus Revelationis* – gives the game away, pointing as it does to the *sources* of revelation, not to its reception. So *Milestones* treats the Vatican conservatives with kid gloves. Second, Ratzinger distances himself from other reformers by lumping them with Geiselmann, and then complaining that he was wrongly identified with this group: 'In the general atmosphere dominant in 1962 . . . it was impossible for me to explain the perspective I had gained from the sources [of tradition] . . . My position was simply aligned with the general opposition to the official schema and considered to be one more vote for Geiselmann.'[7]

Then the attack acquires a personal edge. Turning to the second, more detailed text on revelation that he and Rahner were charged with writing, Ratzinger describes it as 'much more Rahner's work than my own', and says that it drew 'some rather bitter reactions'. As they worked together, *Milestones* suggests, it became obvious to Ratzinger that 'Rahner and I lived on different theological planets.' In fields such as liturgy, the place of biblical commentary in the Church and in theology, 'and in many other areas, he stood for the same things as I did, but for entirely different reasons'.[8] Ratzinger finds that Rahner's theology was 'totally conditioned' by a tradition of scholasticism shaped by Francisco Suárez (1548–1617), the great Spanish Jesuit, 'and its new reception in the light of German idealism and of Heidegger'.

Leaving aside the question of whether justice is done to Rahner by such a sweeping comment, it is again noteworthy that Ratzinger singles out his erstwhile friend and ally for criticism, while avoiding unfavourable comment on conservative approaches that also clashed with his own view at the time. The mystery is deepened by his suggestion that the official text 'was rejected by a narrow margin'. In fact 1,368 votes were cast against the official schema, and 822 in favour of continuing the debate. As reported, *Dei Verbum* was not finally completed until the last days of the Council. In *Milestones*, Ratzinger accepts that it was one of Vatican II's outstanding texts, but cautions that it has yet to be truly received.

Though also tendentious in places, the material on liturgy in *Milestones* can be taken much more at face value. Since Ratzinger was a *ressourcement*-minded Catholic, his reformist instincts were generally governed by the impulse to unearth treasure from the past. Nor does it take a great leap to understand his conclusion (cemented by the late 1960s) that too much had been sacrificed in the democratisation of the liturgy. One of his first comments is that liturgical reform was not a priority for the bishops. Where the subject was raised, notably in France and Germany after the First World War, this had been in the context of a wish to restore the ancient Roman rite, 'to which belonged the active involvement of the people in the liturgical event'. In Ratzinger's understanding, the subject was given an early slot on the Council's agenda only because it was uncontroversial. 'It would not have occurred to any of the Fathers to see in this text a "revolution" signifying the "end of the Middle Ages", as some theologians felt they should interpret it subsequently.'[9] The schema was viewed as moving forward the reforms introduced by Pius X 'and carried on carefully but resolutely' by Pius XII. Ratzinger accepts that some liturgists who advised the bishops had a deeper appetite for reform from the outset. 'Their wishes would surely not have received the approval of the Fathers. Nor were such wishes expressed in any way in the text of the Council, although one can subsequently read them into some general statements.'[10]

One of many snapshots of his later attitudes – and the policies to which they would give rise – comes in his address to a group of traditionalist liturgists at the Ecclesia Dei conference in Rome in October 1998.[11] In areas where the pre-conciliar liturgical movement had 'anticipated the essential ideas of the Council, as for example the praying participation of all', he suggests, 'there was greater suffering in the face of a liturgical reform undertaken in too much haste and limiting itself often to the exterior aspect.' Ratzinger then tells his audience that *Sacrosanctum Concilium* says Latin ought to be preserved while giving greater space to the vernacular, 'especially in the readings and directives, and in some of the prayers and chants'; and he cautions that the document 'does not say a word' about whether the priest should celebrate Mass in the eastward or westward position. There was therefore a dubious warrant for moves towards greater latitude: 'A number of modern liturgists, however, have unfortunately shown a tendency to develop the ideas of the Council in only one direction. If one does this, one ends up reversing the intentions of the Council.'

The speech goes on to enumerate negative consequences of the misapplication of conciliar teaching:

> The role of the priest is reduced by some to one of pure functionality. The fact that the entire Body of Christ is the subject of the liturgy is often deformed to the point that the

local community becomes the self-sufficient subject of the liturgy and distributes the different roles in it. There is also a dangerous tendency to minimise the sacrificial character of the Mass and to cause mystery and the sacred to disappear, under the self-proclaimed imperative of making the liturgy more easily understood. Finally, one notes the tendency to fragment the liturgy and to emphasise only its communal character by giving the assembly the power to decide [on] the celebration.

None of Ratzinger's factual claims here is false (they were also made in an anguished letter which he wrote to Paul VI in October 1972), but the tone of his argument is viewed with surprise by some professional liturgists. An American expert comments that 'the point about *Sacrosanctum Concilium* is that it spells out principles, not detailed policies. Developments such as the westward position were then worked out in detail in the aftermath of Vatican II under Pope Paul.' The sentiments about continuity expressed at the Council 'were partly political', this source adds: 'When change is on the agenda, it's often a good strategy to emphasise continuity with the past.' We shall return to the subject of liturgy in Chapter 7.

* * *

Ratzinger's other major area of consistency – his hostile verdict on *Gaudium et Spes* – has already been outlined. It was to drive a wedge between the *aggiornamento* and *ressourcement* parties, and ultimately expose deeper divisions between the former allies. As Professor Joseph A. Komonchak has recorded in a very astute article for the journal *Commonweal*,[12] *Gaudium et Spes* has an optimistic or 'French' flavour, reflecting the influence of the Dominican theologian, Marie-Dominique Chenu, whose approach was to identify spiritual impulses in the non-believer, and then cultivate them with the Christian message. Chenu termed such impulses *pierres d'attente* (toothing stones, as Komonchak explains, 'that jut out from a wall in order to mesh with an eventual addition'). For its supporters, this approach results in a mature conversation based on respect for the other, and an assumption that the seeds of God's Word extend beyond Christian boundaries. As we have also seen, it could claim an underpinning in the thought of St Thomas Aquinas.

41

Unsurprisingly, Ratzinger saw Chenu's approach as putting the cart before the horse. It neglected the reality of sin, he thought, confused the natural and supernatural, and failed to distinguish properly between the Church and the world. Christian categories were then grafted on to what was essentially sociological analysis; and, as a result, *Gaudium et Spes* formed an instance of 'the fiction that it is possible to construct a rational philosophical picture of man intelligible to all and on which all men of goodwill can agree, the actual Christian doctrines being added to this as a sort of crowning conclusion'.[13] The text should rather have taken as its starting-point 'the actual Christian creed which, precisely as a confession of faith, can and must manifest its own intelligibility and rationality'.

On 18 March 2005, a month and a day before he became Pope, Ratzinger preached in St Peter's Basilica to mark the fortieth anniversary of the publication of *Gaudium et Spes*. His praise for the document was diplomatic rather than heartfelt, and the subtext of the homily obvious. The Church draws enthusiastic praise from the world when she commits herself to justice 'on a human level'. But when church campaigns touch on areas that the world 'no longer sees as bound up with human dignity', such as promoting life from conception to death, 'or when the Church confesses that justice also includes our responsibilities towards God himself', then the world turns cold. The Cardinal concluded that justice, for the Christian, cannot be a worldy category alone.

What sorts of verdict can be drawn at this stage? The most plausible assessment seems to be that the young theologian firmly supported institutional reform and greater intellectual freedom on the one hand, but also felt rising concern that the Church was embracing secular modernity with too much enthusiasm. The second of these instincts would overshadow and ultimately supplant the first, leading to an allied conclusion: that the repatriation of powers to the episcopacy had been a very mixed blessing.

Given that *Milestones* was written during the 1990s, Ratzinger's sombre side holds sway. He records:

More and more the Council appeared to be like a great Church parliament that could change everything and reshape everything according to its own desires. Very clearly resentment was growing against Rome and against the Curia, which appeared

to be the real enemy for everything that was new and progressive. The disputes at the Council were more and more portrayed
according to the party model of modern parliamentarism
. . . The faith no longer seemed exempt from human decision
making but rather was now apparently determined by it.[14]

After the end of the first session, he returned home full of hope
for a new start. But during the course of 1963 and 1964, he would
become 'deeply troubled by the change in ecclesial climate that
was becoming ever more evident'.

Consiliar sessions took place only during the autumn, and so
bishops and their advisers could still spend most of the period
1962–65 on home turf. For Ratzinger, this nevertheless entailed a
good deal of disequilibrium. On the eve of the Council, he was
offered a chair in Christian doctrine (a stronger suit for him than
fundamental theology) at Münster, agonised, and then declined
it. Within a year he had changed his mind, citing the opposition
he encountered in the 'tension-filled' faculty at Bonn, especially
over the examining of two doctoral candidates. Münster appealed
to him as a 'beautiful and noble' place, but he felt homesick at
times, and longed for a chance to return south. His appetite for
another move was sharpened by an incipient conflict with Johann
Baptist Metz, a friend whose appointment to Münster's Catholic
faculty had been secured on his own recommendation. In
Milestones, Ratzinger says rather baldly that Metz's growing interest
in political theology was not to his taste, and that he could see 'a
conflict emerging that could go deep indeed'.[15] An escape route
was provided by the redoubtable Hans Küng, a fellow *peritus* and
friend of Ratzinger before their headlong collision during the
1970s, who helped secure him the offer of a chair at Tübingen, in
Swabia. Ratzinger seized this chance, and moved to one of
Germany's most charming university towns in the summer of
1966.

By this stage – and it was not his final academic post – he had
served in four university faculties in a space of only eight years, a
situation described as 'exceptionally' unusual by other German
scholars. He was certainly an able young man in demand. But the
rapid changes of address also reflect the querulous streak that
had already emerged in his arguments with colleagues. It is hard
not to see a patchwork quality in his character, as well as his
thought.

4

Jumping Ship

As the chronicle of an evolution towards the views which the Cardinal would hold in middle age and beyond, *Milestones* is by definition a progressively more reliable document. Yet even some of the book's closing sections are partial. Among other bits of potentially embarrassing information swept from the record are Ratzinger's membership of the editorial board of *Concilium*, a journal set up in 1965 to promote a progressive interpretation of Vatican II, and his signing, with more than thirteen hundred other Catholic theologians, of the 1968 Nijmegen declaration, that 'the freedom of theologians, and theology in the service of the Church, regained by Vatican II, must not be jeopardised again'. It appeared at the time of Paul VI's restatement of the ban on contraception in *Humanae Vitae*, when many priests and laypeople were leaving the Church in protest. Signatories included Karl Rahner, Edward Schillebeeckx, Yves Congar and Hans Küng. That Ratzinger still had a subversive streak at around the age of 40 is well illustrated in an anecdote told by Professor Wolfgang Beinert, then one of his research students, who had moved to Tübingen after a spell in Italy. 'At a seminar once, Ratzinger asked everyone for their opinion about a problem that had come up,' Beinert told me. 'When it was my turn to speak, Ratzinger said with an ironic smile, "I don't need to ask you; I know what opinion you have to have as a Roman!" '

Overall, however, Ratzinger's outlook was becoming both more conservative and more pessimistic – a fact reflected in his gradual move away from Rahner's orbit towards that of von Balthasar. I have reported that Rahner has a sunnier estimate of human nature, and its orientedness towards divine gace. Unlike the Protestants he admires (especially Karl Barth), von Balthasar sees a half-built bridge towards faith in the human sense of beauty; but in his scheme this impulse is both answered and wholly overturned by the Christian revelation. As Rowan Williams summarises the matter, Rahner's Christ answers our questions; but von Balthasar's questions our answers.[1] Ratzinger increasingly came to believe that there was something too cosy in Rahner's formulation. Von Balthasar's alternative was intellectually more bracing, as well as closer to the heart of tradition.

This, in broad outline, is the theological background against which the trauma Ratzinger suffered in 1968 should be seen. Tübingen was for a time affected by sit-ins and demonstrations, one of which involved the desecration of a crucifix, derided as a badge of sado-masochism. Professor David Martin, a sociologist then teaching at the London School of Economics, remembers a tide of disruption and verbal assaults on lecturers. He says that the position was 'considerably worse' in Germany, where Marxism had become more deeply rooted. On the other hand, Professor Gerald O'Collins SJ of the Gregorian University in Rome recalls a less dramatic situation at Tübingen, where he spent part of each summer during the years 1966–68. 'I got the impression that people were for the most part letting off steam,' he says. 'There was a great deal of talk and not much action.'

But now that the 1960s is often associated with little more than empty-headedness, it is important to fill out the picture. The urge to loosen educational and social fetters was especially powerful in Germany, where young people suspected their elders of promoting a conspiracy of silence about the Nazi period. Whether Ratzinger's response to all this was caused by provocation, or grounded in intellectual misgivings, or merely symptomatic of a flappable personality and hurt pride (German professors could hitherto have counted on their students' deference), his intense distress at the turn of events is beyond doubt, as is the influence it would have on his view of the Church. Within two years, he was once again on the move – this time to the newly established university of Regensburg in Bavaria – after further unhappiness and disputes with colleagues.

To begin with, he was delighted with his new place of work, despite health problems that he ascribed to overwork, and the initial need to travel back and forth to Münster. Tübingen is often described as more like Oxford or Cambridge than any other German seat of learning. The university dominates the surrounding town, famous for its half-timbered and gabled houses in a web of steep alleys. Ratzinger's first home was cramped, but with Hans Küng's help he moved to a more comfortable building next door to Viktoria Freifrau von Gilhausen, a former javelin thrower in Germany's Olympic squad, and much-loved local character. O'Collins was one of her lodgers; he remembers that there was a high-spirited atmosphere during the day (magnified by a posse of dachshunds nicknamed the *Freihunde*), but a strict ban on noise after 9 p.m. Professor Ratzinger went to sleep at this time, in order to rise at 3.30 or 4 a.m. for a long stint at his desk before breakfast.

The year 1967 saw festivities for the 150th anniversary of the founding of Tübingen's Catholic theology faculty; but any euphoria was fleeting. Ratzinger comments that it was the last celebration of its kind 'in the old style': intellectually, the university was about to be shaken 'to its very foundations' by Marxist influence. The Zeitgeist, as he saw it, was a vivid example of how easily theology could be forced onto the Procrustean bed of other disciplines. He adds that Heideggerian existentialism, a potent influence on mid-twentieth-century biblical scholarship, as well as much doctrinal writing, was now discredited at a stroke by Ernst Bloch, a refugee from East Germany. Ratzinger was left aghast by his colleagues' willingness to swim with the tide, and to recast Christian proclamation in a mould of Marxist messianism: 'I myself have seen the frightful face of this atheistic piety unveiled, its psychological terror, the abandon with which every moral consideration could be thrown overboard as a bourgeois residue when the ideological goal was at stake.' This was all bad enough in itself, he continues, 'but it became an unrelenting challenge to the theologian when the ideology is presented in the name of the faith and the Church is used as its instrument'.[2]

Christoph Schwöbel, a Protestant theologian now teaching at Tübingen, sees this comment as very revealing:

> In Ratzinger's eyes, the key point was not so much the various kinds of opposition to professorial authority or to the authority of the Church, but somehow that the core of Catholic belief was being eroded by a foreign ideology. And it could be that his move to the University of Regensburg, where things were much quieter in terms of debate between students and professors, was a way to withdraw from the front line.

Schwöbel has discussed the matter at length with older colleagues, and says that Ratzinger's behaviour seems to have changed 'quite dramatically' at this time:

> A young, friendly, communicative professor turned in on himself and became very dogmatic. Some people, of course, continued to see him as a model of courtesy. This is because he seems to be the kind of person who will really open up to others if he feels they are on his wavelength, but finds it harder to get on with a larger range of characters.[3]

This interpretation rings true, but it leaves open the question whether Ratzinger's response was proportionate. Vatican II, and the 1960s in general, were moments of big change: it was obvious that the dust would take a while to settle. Large questions are at stake here, of course, but O'Collins's comments on Bloch are an instructive counterweight to Ratzinger's:

> The reason for Bloch's expulsion from East Germany was that, as an existentialist Marxist, he was viewed as heretical. His Jewish background was important, and informed his great work *The Principle of Hope*. I was invited to translate this book, which is written in wonderful, poetic German; sadly, I did not have time to do so. Bloch once joked to me that he was an atheist for the sake of God.[4]

Since O'Collins would end up holding a senior post in one of the world's top Catholic universities, we may conclude that dialogue of this kind does not necessarily involve selling the pass.

But Ratzinger's sensitivities were sharpened by seeing the strife at very close range. He was dean of his faculty, and a member of the commission in charge of devising a new constitution for the university. He nevertheless concedes that 'developments were driven in the way I have described' only 'by a small circle of functionaries'. Most of his students remained on an even keel, and he could count on a lecture hall full of attentive listeners. Conditions in the Lutheran faculty were more troubled, on the other hand, and the distressed Catholic made common cause with two conservative Protestants, Wolfgang Beyerhaus and Ulrich Wickert. Wickert had little appetite for remaining in a 'battle zone', and saw an escape route in an invitation to the Kirchliche Hochschule in Berlin.

Ratzinger's chance of escape came in the offer of a chair in dogma at Regensburg. Before this move (and much of the strife that occasioned it), he produced his best-known book, *Introduction to Christianity*, a series of reflections on the Apostles' Creed for students 'of all faculties'. Mostly written in 1967, it is a full-bodied account of belief that still shows some debt to Rahner, as well as to von Balthasar. Take the following passages. The first comes in the context of a discussion of the Trinity:

> The point at issue . . . is whether man in his relations with God is only dealing with the reflections of his own consciousness or whether it is given to him to reach out beyond himself and to encounter God . . . If the first hypothesis is true, then prayer too is only an occupation of man with himself; there are no more grounds for worship proper than there are for prayers of petition . . . [But] if the other answer is the correct one, prayer and worship are not only possible; they are enjoined . . .

This is the lesson Ratzinger had culled from the Augustinian tradition: if we are created, it is reasonable to believe that humanity is endowed with the means of engaging with ultimate reality. But faith is not necessarily a leap into the dark. Quoting Isaiah 7:9 ('But if you do not stand by me, you will not stand at all.') Ratzinger glosses faith as a matter of 'entrusting oneself to that which has not been made by oneself and never could be made, and which, for that very reason, supports and renders possible all our making'.[5]

The discussion turns to Old Testament faith in Yahweh, a name which Ratzinger (showing a debt to the scholarship of Henri Cazelles) sees as denoting both timeless power and personal self-bestowal. This is held to be picked up in Isaiah 48:12 ('I am He, I am the first and I am the last'), and applied to Jesus in the Johannine sections of the New Testament:

> The formula which first occurs in the episode of the burning bush, which at the end of the Exile becomes the expression of hope and certainty in the face of the declining gods and depicts Yahweh's lasting victory over all these powers, now finds itself here too at the centre of the faith, but through becoming

testimony to Jesus of Nazareth . . . The name is no longer merely a word but a person: Jesus himself.[6]

Christ is thus identified as the human face of God.

This provides a bedrock for the incarnational teaching developed in *Introduction to Christianity*. Ratzinger's trinitarian perspective derives from mainstream tradition, and partly entails reflection on what has been called the 'grammar' of God: if the ground of creation is *eternal* love, it has no need for an object outside itself; and if it is eternal *love*, it must be in some sense relational. To speak of God as Father, Son and Holy Spirit is therefore more than a matter of symbolism. The doctrine of the Trinity entails a claim about the divine nature as well.

* * *

Ratzinger knew that Regensburg should be his final academic berth, and in the absence of ecclesiastical preferment, the place where he should see out his career. This old imperial city on the Danube was beautiful – it had escaped war damage – and tranquil. Ratzinger comments that 'the waves of Marxist revolt' were breaking around even this young university, and there were still 'many determined leftists' among the ranks of the junior lecturers. This was small beer, though, compared with the situation at Tübingen. Regensburg was now also home to Georg, who had recently been appointed director of music at the cathedral there. During the 1970s, Ratzinger acquired a house at Pentling, a village 6 km from the university, with the royalties earned on *Introduction to Christianity*. After he and his sister moved to Rome, they would return there frequently for summer holidays.

Being a new foundation, Regensburg University was still only half-built when the professor arrived, and the theology faculty temporarily operated out of a former Dominican house of studies. Ratzinger comments that there was no shortage of arguments within the department, but that they always took place within a context of mutual respect. The civil atmosphere was self-perpetuating. Doctoral candidates were drawn in numbers from beyond Bavaria, and even outside Germany. One of the overseas students, Joseph Fessio, came from the United States via France to research a thesis on von Balthasar, and has been a fervent admirer of Ratzinger ever since. 'He's gracious, he's gentle, he's soft-spoken,' Fr Fessio told an audience of students just after Ratzinger became Pope. 'I've never heard him say a word in anger, and I've seen him in situations which would make even a meek man angry. Everybody who has ever worked with him and been close to him reveres him as a saint.' Fessio went on to describe the widely praised teaching skills of his former supervisor: '[H]e'll listen for an hour, not taking any notes, and then he'll sum up in one or two long complex German sentences that are beautifully crafted. He'll get at the essence of the whole conversation and weave it all together into [a] summary. He's got this very synthetic mind . . .'[7]

Introduction to Christianity again won its author attention in high places. When people expressed surprise at his appointment as Archbishop of Munich in 1977, others had a ready explanation. Pope Paul had loved Professor Ratzinger's book. Other academic laurels came his way. Paul had set up a Synod of Bishops after Vatican II to sustain the vision of collegiality, and an analogous body, the International Theological Commission (ITC), which was intended to work alongside (or, as some hoped, rein in) the CDF. Ratzinger was among the ITC's first members. Though certain theologians outside its ranks expected the commission to promote liberal causes, he says, it was a relief for him to discover that his colleagues were for the most part erstwhile reformers now concerned that liberty had given way to a free-for-all, both inside and outside the Church. The giants of this group were Henri de Lubac (who, Ratzinger admits in *Milestones*, 'had suffered so much under the narrowness of the [pre-conciliar] neo-scholastic regime') and Hans Urs von Balthasar. Other members included Jorge Medina Estévez, the Chilean who later became Prefect of the Congregation for Divine Worship, and Louis Bouyer, a patristics scholar and leading French authority on Newman. Ratzinger pays tribute to all these people, remarking that he 'cannot even begin'[8] to express his debt to de Lubac and von Balthasar, and also praises the bridge-building skills of Yves Congar. His only target of criticism in this context is Rahner, whom he accuses of being in hock to 'progressive slogans' and 'adventuresome'[9] political positions. (Rahner later resigned from the ITC, alleging that it had failed to fulfil its promise.)

Again, the account given in *Milestones* of what happened next needs to be treated with caution. We are told that von Balthasar wished to found a new journal reflecting the traditionalist vision, and gathered round him a group who (in Ratzinger's words) did not want to do theology 'on the present goals of ecclesial politics but who were intent on developing theology rigorously on the basis of its own proper sources and methods'.[10] The journal, *Communio*, was published in many languages, and actively supported by other heavyweights such as Karl Lehmann, and Walter Kasper (both future cardinals) and Hans Maier, the Bavarian Minister of Culture. Ratzinger served on its board from 1972. As we have seen, he makes no mention of his attachment to *Concilium*, nor that the founding of *Communio* was prompted partly by a disaffected element at *Concilium*. But *Milestones* gives a candid diagnosis of *Communio*'s weaknesses, which are said to include a tendency to academic navel-gazing, and a failure to make a timely response to challenges thrown up by the broader culture.

He also became involved in the Gustav Siewerth Akademy, an independent educational project, at this time. Inspired by the example of Romano Guardini (who had created a centre for spiritual formation among the young during the 1920s and 30s), Ratzinger concluded that his teaching work would be less influential if confined to a university setting. He teamed up with Heinrich Schlier, a biblical scholar, to give residential courses in theology at the academy every summer from 1970 to 1977. A student contact had the use of a newly refurbished building near Lake Constance, and this proved an ideal setting. Young people and lecturers flourished in a convivial atmosphere.

The most significant event in the Church for Ratzinger during his Regensburg period was the publication of the Missal of Paul VI. It draws a renewed *cri de cœur* at the end of *Milestones*. Unlike the Tridentine Missal, Ratzinger felt, which reflected a much more nuanced relationship with earlier forms of the Eucharist, and allowed for the retention of various other long-established rites side by side with the *Missale Romanum*, the new liturgy was like an entirely different structure erected on the site of a demolished building. He does not doubt that the new forms brought many improvements, but judges that 'setting it as a new construction over against what has grown historically . . . has caused us enormous harm'. He deplores the loss: 'When liturgy is self-made . . . it can no longer give us what its proper gift should be: the encounter with the mystery that is not our own product but rather our origin and the source of our life.'[11] He concludes with a call for a new liturgical movement to implement the 'real' heritage of Vatican II.

Ratzinger also produced a study of eschatology (Christian teaching on the ultimate destiny of humanity and the rest of the created order) at this time. Entitled *Eschatology: Death and Eternal Life*, it is his most substantial piece of research, and the work in which he takes most pride as a theologian. Blending biblical, historical and philosophical scholarship, the book asks what the basis of Christian hope is in the face of, on the one hand, widespread scepticism about religious claims, and, on the other, the influence of wordly forms of messianic vision on much theology. Ratzinger sees 'gleams of real gold' in the liberationist vision, but insists that the gospel message of hope is irreducibly supernatural: 'The Kingdom of God, not being itself a political concept, cannot serve as a political criterion by which to construct in direct fashion a programme of political action and to criticise the political efforts of other people.'[12]

He then suggests that modern society trivialises death in opposed but related ways – by sweeping it under the carpet in some contexts, and by making a spectacle of it in some forms of popular entertainment. His argument is distilled by the Dominican theologian Aidan Nichols in his study of Ratzinger's thought:

> whereas people used to pray for deliverance from sudden and [unexpected] death, a contemporary Litany of the Unbelievers would ask for just the opposite: a way of dying that left them no time for reflection or suffering. Alas: when things reach such a pass that accepting death in a human way becomes too danger-ous, being human itself has become too dangerous as well. Perhaps the perplexity to which positivism and materialism thus bring us will at least encourage us to seek out what may be the 'wisdom of the tradition' on the matter.[13]

Ratzinger conveys an essential point about the Christian rationale for life after death: that it isn't a function of something in human beings which survives, but an inference about God. Christians believe that since God's relation to humanity is one of commitment, then it must be counter-intuitive to believe that a line is drawn at our physical death. Amid much else, the book proceeds to see the incarnation, Passion and resurrection as pivotal to the consummation of all things, not just to human history: 'the paschal sacrifice abides in him as an enduring presence. For this reason Heaven, as our becoming one with Christ, takes on the nature of adoration. All cult prefigures it, and in it comes to completion. Christ is the temple of the final age; he is heaven, the new Jerusalem; he is the cultic space for God.'[14]

Eschatology: Death and Eternal Life was to have formed one of several volumes on doctrine which Ratzinger hoped to write in the stable setting to which he had become attached, but the plan was swept aside by his appointment to the episcopacy. The serving Archbishop of Munich, Cardinal Julius Döpfner, died suddenly in July 1976, and at first Ratzinger discounted rumours that he was a likely successor, citing poor health, as well as his scholarly commitments. When the apostolic nuncio offered him the job, he was allowed to consult his confessor, who urged him to accept.

* * *

The new Archbishop was consecrated on 28 May, the vigil of Pentecost, 1977. Ratzinger's pre-installation nervousness abated as large crowds appeared on the streets of Munich to greet him; he recalls the occasion as 'intensely joyful'. Within a month he had also received his cardinal's hat in Rome. As an episcopal motto he chose the phrase 'Co-worker of the Truth' from the Third Letter of John. By tradition, the Archbishop's coat of arms included a crowned Moor, believed to be an emblem of Christian universality. Ratzinger selected two further motifs: a shell, symbolising pilgrimage, and a bear, representing a beast of burden. (According to legend, St Corbinian, first Bishop of Freising, punished a ferocious bear by making it haul a heavy pack all the way to Rome.) Ratzinger ends *Milestones* with a nod to Augustine's insight that a theologian does not foresake his vocation in becoming a bishop. 'Just as a draft animal is closest to the farmer . . . so is Augustine closest to God precisely through . . . humble service.'[15]

How far did the reality match with the pious sentiment over the ensuing four years? We do not possess a detailed account by Ratzinger himself of his time in Munich. The sources are also thinner, because the diocesan clergy are in the main very reluctant to voice criticisms on the record, or even to speak at all, of a former overseer who is now in a position of supreme spiritual authority. But the big picture is both clear and unsurprising, given the arc of Ratzinger's development during the early 1970s. He elicited some very mixed reactions.

Certainly, there were well-informed figures in the diocese who felt that he was very good at his job. In an as yet unpublished essay, his former Vicar-General, Fr Gerhard Gruber, writes that the Archbishop impressed people on all sides with his modesty and warmth. Döpfner's were large shoes for Ratzinger to step into: the older man had been respected for his common touch and skill at the card table. But the new incumbent had at least one major advantage over his twentieth-century predecessors. None of them had been a native Bavarian. And although academia was a world away from the concerns of most laypeople, it had at least given Ratzinger many opportunities for cultivating ties with Protestants. As a result, ecumenical relations improved substantially during his time.

The Munich diocese consists of 750 parishes serving two million souls. Gruber describes Ratzinger's regular round of parish visits as the highlight of his routine, and his ex officio work on numerous committees as 'far less pleasant'. Early assumptions that the Archbishop would be an aloof figure were soon dispelled, Gruber maintains. His addresses were simple and to the point, fuelling the sense that they came from someone 'personally addressed by God'. Younger members of his flock are said to have been especially impressed, and at one point clubbed together to buy their chief pastor a live bear. Gruber ends his testimony on a reverent note: Ratzinger's 'first and last words' as Archbishop of Munich 'concerned the peace of Christ, and it would seem that this will also be the main theme of his pontificate'.

This interpretation is qualified by another priest who held a senior post in the diocese during the late 1970s, but did not wish to be named. 'Ratzinger's relations with me and my brother clergy were cordial but not that warm,' he comments. 'The Cardinal was a scholar. He gave the impression of living inside his head. Administration was not his strong suit, and that burden tended to be shouldered by others.' The point is developed by Wolfgang Beinert, who went on to become a professor at Regensburg. 'When Ratzinger left the university, a valedictory dinner was held at which he stood up and said to the assembled company: "Until now I have sat with you on one side of the table. Now I am moving to the other side." This took us aback.'

Joseph Ratzinger in military uniform, 1943

The Ratzinger family in 1951 (left to right):
Maria, Georg, Maria Sr, Joseph and Joseph Sr

The recently ordained priest celebrating an outdoor Mass in 1952

Lecturing at the seminary in Freising, 1955

Ratzinger during the 1970s

Cardinal Ratzinger greets Pope John Paul II in December 2003

The Cardinal two months before his election as Pope

Habemus Papam: 19 April 2005

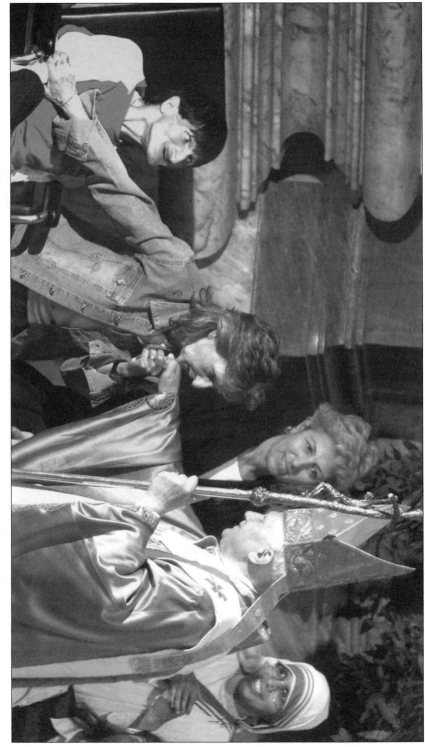

Pope Benedict is greeted by the sick after his inaugural Mass, 24 April 2005

The bookies' favourites (top row): Jorge Mario Bergoglio (Buenos Aires), Angelo Scola (Venice); (second row): Dionigi Tettamanzi (Milan), Ivan Dias (Mumbai); (bottom row): Joseph Ratzinger, Carlo Maria Martini

Pope Benedict outside his former home, on the day after his election

More generally, Beinert judges, Ratzinger has long suffered from 'a lack of *Menschenkenntnis*' – the capacity to size people up. 'He's not good at tailoring what he says to different kinds of audience, despite his professed concern for simple believers.' This suggestion was repeated to me time and again, including by one priest who felt that a verdict once delivered on the young Ratzinger by a Jesuit, Fr Karl Adolf Kreuser, had remained true thereafter. 'Kreuser said that Ratzinger was too tense and anxious to make a good parish priest. I don't think that the situation changed much as the years went by.' Another cleric who did not want to be named for fear of penalties provided an example of the Archbishop's questionable pastoral skills. 'I know a priest who contacted Ratzinger in October one year to request an urgent meeting. Ratzinger replied that the next available slot in his diary was the following March.'

Word got round the diocese about a meeting Ratzinger once had with the Jesuit Provincial, Fr Alfons Klein, a Bavarian of his own age who had left the seminary to join the German resistance to the Nazis at the end of the war. The Provincial said, 'Your Eminence, do you have any complaints against the Jesuits in Munich?' 'No', came the reply. The Provincial was just leaving the room when Ratzinger suddenly declared that he'd had complaints that a Fr Bernd Knüfer was in the habit of celebrating Mass without the proper vestments. The Provincial was surprised, but promised to investigate. It later emerged that the complaint was groundless. 'But Ratzinger never apologised, and this was interpreted as a mark of petulance,' according to my source. 'I was at a meeting of clergy when the announcement of his departure to Rome was made. I'm afraid that the news prompted an eruption of cheering.'

Not that his absence removed his influence. The sense that he was a poor judge of character would continue to be felt over the decades ahead, because of his membership of the Vatican congregation dealing with episcopal appointments. 'Despite his politeness in many situations, there's a kind of paranoia there too,' one German journalist told me. 'Hotheads have on occasion made unfounded accusations against good men, and Ratzinger has not had the sense to discount such complaints.' The point was echoed by a respected religious affairs commentator, Daniel Deckers of the *Frankfurter Allgemeine Zeitung*. 'Ratzinger's influence on the Catholic Bishops' Conference in Germany has been very problematic,' he told me. 'The effect of his interventions has been that second-rate men have regularly achieved promotion, and first-rate men have been held back.'

No such doubts about Ratzinger's abilities were felt in Rome, where he took part in two conclaves within four months of joining the College of Cardinals, and served as papal legate at a Marian congress in Ecuador. The death of John Paul I (Albino Luciani, formerly Patriarch of Venice) on 29 September 1978 after only a month in office was seen by some as a reproach to the caution displayed by the electors; and several influential figures, including Franz König, the Austrian Primate, began canvassing for a non-Italian candidate. This remained an unlikely option, according to well-placed contemporary sources such as Peter Hebblethwaite and Tad Szulc. In their view, Karol Wojtyla emerged victorious in part because voters were deadlocked over the competing claims of two Italians (Giovanni Benelli, Archbishop of Florence, and Giuseppe Siri, the ultra-conservative Archbishop of Genoa); and because an efficient campaign was orchestrated by several opinion-formers, including the Archbishop of Philadelphia, John Krol – and Ratzinger himself – to deliver the votes of their respective countrymen. Though Ratzinger had met Wojtyla only a month beforehand, some of the sentiments expressed by the Archbishop of Munich in pre-conclave interviews are revealing in hindsight. He hoped the successful candidate would hold the line against liberation theology, and substitute something more confrontational for *Ostpolitik* – the Vatican's accommodation with Eastern-bloc countries shaped by Pope Paul and his Secretary of State, Agostino Casaroli.

Ratzinger's high regard for the Pope from Poland was reciprocated. John Paul II had also read and greatly admired *Introduction to Christianity*, and recognised that its author's theological pedigree was richer than his own. He wanted Ratzinger on the inside track, and in 1979 offered to make him Prefect of the Vatican Congregation for Catholic Education. The Cardinal declined, saying that he had not been long enough in Munich.

His three remaining years as a diocesan bishop saw further controversy. In 1979, the university senate in Munich unanimously chose J. B. Metz's name from a shortlist of three to succeed Professor Heinrich Freis in the chair of dogma. Exercising a power available to him under the Bavarian Concordat, Ratzinger asked his friend Hans Maier to veto Metz and appoint another candidate, Heinrich Döring. The move gave widespread offence in Germany, and drew a sharp rebuke from Karl Rahner, who accused Ratzinger of bad faith in an open letter to him. 'Is Metz unorthodox or immoral?' Rahner asked. 'If so, why has no accusation been made against him all these years? I can only suppose that the reason is your personal opposition to Metz's political theology.' Rahner went on to say that he himself had been forbidden to write on the subject of eucharistic concelebration during the 1950s: 'That was a senseless, unscientific manipulation by church bureaucrats. I judge your action against Metz to be of the same category.'[16] Ratzinger's breach with Rahner was never healed (the latter died in 1984), but cordial relations were restored with Metz during the 1990s.

As we have seen, a foretaste of Ratzinger's style at the CDF was given by his part in the campaign against Hans Küng, whose *missio canonica*, or licence to teach Catholic theology, was withdrawn in 1979. Küng is almost the same age as Ratzinger, and they are probably the two best-known Catholic theologians of their generation. But Küng became an increasingly outspoken critic of official church teaching after the Council. His admirers hail him as a prophet; traditionalists reply that a theologian has no warrant to say, at length and in public, that he is right and the Church wrong about important articles of belief. The matter is complicated by Küng's weakness for self-promotion. He has an unusually high profile for a academic, and many of his campaigns have been conducted through the mass media.

Early in his career, Küng was even more precocious than Ratzinger, because his doctorate made waves outside university circles through its argument that Protestant and Catholic teaching on justification are in substance the same. A fundamental source of division between the Western Churches appeared to be swept aside at a stroke. His forthright style got him into trouble at some points during Vatican II: *My Struggle for Freedom*,[17] the first volume of his autobiography, contains a memorable vignette about his being summoned before Cardinal Ottaviani. Undaunted, however, he went on to criticise Vatican centralism in his book *The Church*. This prompted the CDF to open a file on him. In 1970, he raised the stakes further in his book *Infallible? An Enquiry*, which argued *inter alia* that the doctrine in question cannot mean that individuals are incapable of erring. Rather, he argued, it is based on Christ's promise that the Church should not fail. Küng warned against ideas about infallibility that appear to rule out a place for doubt or debate; and he fleshed out his case with a rehearsal of how the Church had been all too prone to wrongdoing for much of its history.

The book led to an investigation by the German Bishops' Conference, and was censured by academic reviewers, including Ratzinger and Rahner. Four years later, Küng published *On Being a Christian*, a best-selling work of apologetics. For all its popularity with general readers, this book also received some savage notices from traditionalists: Ratzinger described its theology as 'rootless and ultimately nonbinding', and charged Küng with 'undisguised arrogance'. In a reply to this review, penned for the *Frankfurter Allgemeine Zeitung* in May 1976, Küng accused his former colleague of 'innumerable misrepresentations' of his position.

A flurry of meetings and correspondence about the dissident took place over the following months, but by 1978, the bishops believed that they had a gentlemen's agreement with Küng that he would not intervene further in the infallibility debate. They felt betrayed when, in 1979, he wrote an introduction to a book on the subject by August Bernhard Hasler; and after a meeting in Rome involving John Paul II, Ratzinger and other cardinals, German church officials announced on 18 December that Küng's licence was being revoked.

Ratzinger returned to prominence a few months later in Rome when John Paul made him *relator* of the Synod on the Family, which saw a reaffirmation of the Vatican's hard line against contraception and marriage after divorce. He was considered a capable and efficient chairman, but over-zealous, to some, in seeking outcomes palatable to the Curia. For example, he tried to impose a draft of the final report on the participating bishops, but the preference among the majority was for allowing material to emerge organically from their own deliberations. Their eventual judgements were nevertheless in line with official teaching.

The intense disappointment felt by bishops hoping for a more open process (it was their first opportunity to debate *Humanae Vitae* at an official level) can be illustrated with reference to the Synod's leading English participant, Cardinal Basil Hume. He and the Archbishop of Liverpool, Derek Worlock, had supported a National Pastoral Congress earlier in 1980, and listened open-mindedly as laypeople aired their misgivings about the letter of church rules on sexual ethics. Delegates had gone on to appeal for a 'development' of this teaching. Hume later met John Paul in private, presented him with a report on the congress, open at the two pages on contraception, and asked him to read it. The Pope took the document, but put it to one side.[18]

Hume's take on events in the synod hall afterwards is worth quoting in more detail, because of what it reveals about the world in which Ratzinger would shortly assume a position of great importance. As one of his obituarists reported in 1999, Hume

> made a memorable contribution, saying that in a dream he had seen that the insight behind *Humanae Vitae*, confirming the traditional teaching of the Church, was surely right. But the Church was like a pilgrim, searching for the way. There were signposts to help it. 'The right signs point the way, but signposts become weather-beaten and new paint is needed . . . My dream became a nightmare, for I saw the wrong paint being put upon the signposts, and the last state was worse than the first.'[19]

Worlock attempted to raise the question of the pastoral treatment of divorced people who married again. Hume did not feel afterwards that the concerns of the Catholic community of England and Wales had been given a fair hearing. His style of leadership was thereafter more defensive, and much concerned with protecting his flock from the hand of Rome, as his subsequent tussle with CDF officials, reported in Chapter 7, makes clear.

* * *

A small blemish in relations between Ratzinger and Vatican officials occurred soon after the synod, when John Paul made a pastoral visit to Bavaria. At an open-air Mass in Theresienwiese, near Munich, a victory for free speech was chalked up. Barbara Engl, a social worker, was billed to greet the Pope on behalf of local young people; and her text (which had been drawn up in consultation with Ratzinger's staff) made reference to negative perceptions about official teaching. 'Young people in Germany cannot understand why, despite the drastic shortage of priests, the Church clings unyieldingly to the celibacy rule,' Engl said. She went on to plead for more church offices to be opened to women, and for a more tolerant ecclesiastical climate generally. 'In order to tackle the many questions and problems in the Church, in society and in the world, young people need the trust of those who are ordained. They need credible dialogue partners and people who take their wishes, fears, hopes and commitment seriously.'

John Paul was evidently horrified by these remarks, and Ratzinger claimed that he had been tricked, after insisting beforehand that the offending material be excised from the text. Engl denied any bad faith, protesting that the instruction had never been passed on to her. She then sought meetings with Ratzinger on several occasions during the months that followed, but was cold-shouldered. Within a year of this episode, the Cardinal was packing his bags for the move that would bring his rootless habit of life to an end.

5

The Prefect's Project:
An Overview

Ratzinger's existence over his 23 years as Prefect was outwardly undramatic. He did not travel much, apart from visits to Pentling and Scheyern, a monastery near Munich that hosted his annual retreat. He walked most mornings from his flat, opposite the Vatican, to his office in the Sant'Uffizio, a quadrangle just south of St Peter's Square. (As his fame grew, and pilgrims in large numbers began approaching him for a blessing, he opted to be chauffeured to work.) Most of his evenings were spent in his own household, run by Maria Ratzinger, and, after her death, by Dr Ingrid Stampa, a German musicologist now in her fifties. The Cardinal would relax with his beloved cats, with a post-prandial cigarette, or at the piano. He reveres Bach, and loves Mozart, above all other composers.

This picture perhaps belies the great authority Ratzinger possessed. He would in due course become the weightiest figure in the Catholic Church after the Pope, with a position on several Vatican bodies besides the CDF, including the Congregation for Divine Worship, the Congregation for Education, and the Congregation for the Oriental Churches, as well as the Congregation for Bishops. He had set a crucial condition when offered the post of Prefect – to be allowed to continue writing. Being a far more formidable theologian than his recent predecessors, he had no wish to be straitjacketed in the role of judge. Liberal critics of his tenure at the CDF tend to base their view on reservations about his combined status as referee and player.

John Paul over-ruled him only on a handful of occasions; otherwise the two worked hand in glove together. They met alone every Friday evening unless one or other was away, and did not confine their exchanges to CDF business. The philosopher-Pope invariably wanted to know the mind of the theologian-Cardinal on other questions. They communicated in a mixture of German and Italian. (Like many educated Germans of his generation, Ratzinger has excellent French and decent English. He did not speak the local language on arriving in Rome, but soon mastered it thoroughly. Later he learnt Spanish, and usually conversed with visiting Hispanic bishops in their own tongue – though they were implored to speak *lentamente*.)

That the Prefect was at an ecclesiastical nerve centre is not to say that he could act as he chose – or that his image as a contemporary Grand Inquisitor isn't a caricature. When asked how he could guarantee the objectivity of CDF decisions, he answered that he was no more than a steward:

> The first guarantee is that we don't simply invent anything ourselves but work within the great ideas of the faith. The second is that we consult widely when we make practical applications, and we don't adopt isolated opinions or make decisions until a convergence has emerged among a represent-ative circle of consultors. What is important is that we don't go beyond what is already present in the faith – which naturally has to be applied – and that we then see that a . . . consensus emerges.[1]

These words are largely dependable, and should be seen in the light of a comment already noted about Ratzinger's personal style. Groups of bishops from overseas were sometimes talked down to ('treated like altar boys', in a famous complaint of Cardinal Joseph Bernadin of Chicago) by the staff at other Vatican departments. Some of Ratzinger's lieutentants were also rude on occasion, but the Prefect himself made people feel cherished. He was also liked for his benign humour, according to Fr Augustine Di Noia OP, a current CDF official. 'There was a lot of laughter around the office,' he told me, 'especially about the constant dramas in the world of Italian politics.'

Later parts of this chapter will explore cavils about the Congregation in some detail, so it seems fitting to elaborate the case for the defence at this stage. Much of the material on both sides of the argument comes from anonymous sources who had dealings with the CDF in their capacities as religious superiors or bishops directly responsible for the theologians under investigation. The unwillingness of most to be named is itself a sign of the wintry atmosphere in parts of the Church these days. But it also reflects concern for the privacy of those under their oversight. And sometimes, of course, a comment is all the more to the point for being off the record.

Ratzinger's argument quoted above overlaps a good deal with the view of Timothy Radcliffe, Master of the Dominican order for most of the 1990s. 'Modern liberal society has a big problem with the concept of censorship,' he told me. 'But if someone denies a core belief such as the resurrection or the divinity of Jesus, I don't think that there's anything tyrannical in saying that he or she cannot teach their views in the name of the Church. This isn't a limitation on free speech. People are perfectly free to express their opinion; but it is proper that the authorities can say, "Well, if you do argue such-and-such, we're not going to expel you from our ranks, but we *can* declare that in so teaching, you are not teaching the faith of the Church." ' An apparently open-and-shut case often cited is that of Roger Haight, an American Jesuit whose views appear to lean towards Unitarianism. His right to teach in a Catholic university was taken away in early 2005 after a lengthy Vatican investigation. Defenders of this penalty have a clear argument: if the Catholic Church takes institutional responsibility for what its teachers say, then it has to be sure that their teaching is authentic.

A further general consideration concerns CDF machinery. The Inquisition of earlier centuries was often passive or sluggish, as well as punitive, and observers believe that the first two attributes have continued as much as the third into the present day. One senior source distinguishes between two ways in which a probe from the Congregation might develop. 'In one kind of instance, you find a bishop or superior thwarting an investigation by replying that he or she will deal with it themselves. They say, "It's my responsibility"; and for the most part Ratzinger was happy to let them get on with it. There were other ways of kicking a subject into the long grass. A famous priest once provoked heavy criticism from the CDF for a frank interview he had given to a Dutch newspaper. His superior wrote to Ratzinger saying that he was surprised the Cardinal put so much trust in the evidence of the press. The CDF never replied.' Another observer in Rome makes an entertaining point about the guile that can be shown by objects of the CDF's attentions. 'I know some members of one order who discovered that the Congregation automatically sends out fresh letters if it has not received an answer to a query after six months. By always replying to correspondence two days before this interval had elapsed, they managed to send the CDF computer system into disarray.'

A related kind of outcome identified by one of my contacts reminds one of the Court of Chancery in *Bleak House*. 'Some investigations would drag on for years and years,' he said, 'before eventually ending in a kind of stalemate. There was enormous frustration in the case of one major theologian, because Ratzinger said that the CDF wanted to clarify issues in his ecclesiology. So the theologian's superior asked what these issues were; and the Cardinal didn't seem to know. Ratzinger said then, and on a number of other occasions *sotto voce*, that he wasn't very impressed with the quality of certain members of his staff, and that he needed better theologians. The trouble is that many of the guys who would be good staff members have no wish to work for the Congregation; and many of those who do want to work there wouldn't be suitable. So there is a real difficulty.'

These sentiments were backed up by another senior figure of great experience. 'Ratzinger's deputies included Alberto Bovone [1984–1995] and Tarcisio Bertone [1995–2002]. Bertone [now Archbishop of Genoa] is able, but can be quick-tempered. Bovone simply hadn't mastered his brief some of the time. On one occasion, a religious superior told him that the answer to his query was plain to see, on the next page of the document being discussed. Bovone's failure to understand the detail of the case was obvious. He was so humiliated that he ended up in tears.' More generally, this source adds, 'the model for the appraisal of a theologian's work has shifted over recent decades from that of the law court to something more akin to the examination of a thesis. An examiner is a judge and jury rolled into one. He holds all the cards; and that is less satisfactory when someone's good name is at stake.'

* * *

The Congregation consists of about twenty senior prelates from around the world, most of them cardinals, who convene every 18 months or so to oversee general areas of policy. Roughly forty members of staff – administrators, theologians and upwardly mobile clerical bureaucrats – are responsible for day-to-day operations. Comparisons between the CDF and Orwell's Big Brother are therefore misplaced. As the Dominican Fergus Kerr once remarked, 'the office staff of the municipal cleansing department in a town the size of Oxford is as big as, and certainly far better paid than, the officials of the CDF.'[2] The most senior figures below the Prefect are the Secretary (usually an archbishop) and the Under-Secretary; they and their colleagues are advised by an ad hoc group of experts, for the most part professors at Rome's pontifical universities, and by members of the International Theological Commission. For much of Ratzinger's time as Prefect, the CDF covered several areas besides doctrine, including applications for marriage annulments, and requests from clergy seeking to return to secular life.

The subject of a doctrinal investigation will almost certainly be a priest, religious or lay employee of a Catholic university. Lay theologians in secular seats of learning are beyond the reach of formal discipline. Most complaints against individuals are sent to the Congregation by traditionalists, who naturally worry more about perceived defilement of belief than those favouring greater pluralism. The CDF is obliged to look into all accusations that are not self-evidently specious, though in practice formal proceedings are unlikely to be launched without the agreement of the relevant bishop or religious superior. Debate about the alleged high-handedness of the Congregation therefore has less to do with how many cases are investigated than with how many are dropped. Figures are unavailable, but the answer to this second question, as we have seen, is 'a significant number'. The Congregation's tight-lipped stance about statistics is often defended as a mark of good manners, rather than anything more sinister. A theologian cleared of any unorthodox leanings may find that mud sticks, if the process has taken place in public. Better, say officials, that he or she should have no knowledge of an investigation, since it may well be shelved at an early stage.

A complaint deemed to have substance will be passed up the chain of command, and if the Prefect agrees that there is a prima facie case to be answered, the details of the theologian under investigation will be farmed out to an individual official, who will take charge of practical details. If, after a further interval, the

Congregation collectively confirms its decision to proceed against someone, he or she might be asked to submit 'clarifications' to Rome, or else a bishop or superior might be asked to launch disciplinary action under his or her own steam. If further action is judged necessary after that, the Congregation launches an 'ordinary examination', under which CDF consultors read and report on a subject's work, and a *relatore pro auctore* (a kind of advocate for the accused) is appointed to speak in his or her defence. If officials – acting together in a committee known as the 'particular congress' – decide to pursue a case further, it is put before a formal meeting of the Congregation's members (or as many as are in Rome on the date concerned). To be carried further, a decision of the CDF to proceed against a theologian must be endorsed by the Pope. If, after further stages, a theologian is judged guilty of heresy or one of several lesser offences, the range of penalties at the Congregation's disposal includes excommunication, the withdrawal of the *missio canonica*, a period of 'penitential silence', and a ban (usually temporary) on publishing and public speaking. CDF statutes decree that priests failing to yield at this stage may be deprived of their status, and religious may be expelled from their communities.

If the profile of the Congregation between 1982 and 2005 were judged simply by how much use was made of the stiffest penalties, then one might conclude that Ratzinger had taken a relaxed approach to doctrinal enforcement. Apart from Küng, the American moral theologian Charles Curran, and the Brazilian liberation theologian Leonardo Boff, very few people were stripped of the *missio canonica*; and the only rebel to incur excommunication (lifted after several months) was Fr Tissa Balasuriya, a Sri Lankan priest, in 1997. Virtually unknown outside theological circles, Balasuriya had questioned the tenability of belief in original sin and Catholic teaching about the Virgin Mary. Even most of his supporters accepted that there was a case to answer, but protested that a sledgehammer was being taken to a nut. The following year the Belgian Jesuit Jacques Dupuis, a far more substantial figure, was accused of denying the definitiveness of Christian revelation in his book *Toward a Christian Theology of Religious Pluralism*.[3] The most serious charges against him were eventually dropped after a sometimes heavy-handed investigation of his work. Most famously, Boff got into hot water after complaints about his ecclesiology and debt to Marxism. Significantly, however, it was he who had appealed to Ratzinger for support in the first place. The initiative for an ultimately momentous case did not lie in Rome.

Seen in isolation, though, these cases give little sense of the broader environment. The point, argues Professor Curran, 'is that the Vatican authorities chose areas of study, and geographical areas, to make examples of people: Küng in Europe on the Church; myself in America on sexual ethics; Boff because he was from Brazil, which is the country where liberation theology was most influential, and Dupuis and Balasuriya on interfaith dialogue. As a result, a chill factor has indeed arisen in places where Catholic theology is taught. In the States, for example, people know that they must not question official teaching on sex, because of what happened to me.'

Another cause of the falling temperature arose from the CDF's lower-level forms of discipline. Ratzinger did not merely launch lengthy investigations; he also wrote frequent letters to bishops in dioceses where conservatives had reported alleged irregularities. 'Bishop Franz Kamphaus of Limburg, near Frankfurt, was on the receiving end of much panicky correspondence,' a German source told me. 'At one point, Ratzinger was writing to him almost every month. Among his complaints was that large numbers of men had been seen attending a regular Mass at a certain church. The Cardinal wanted to know whether this was a planned event for gay Catholics.'

One of my other interviewees (a lay German theologian) said that the CDF had sabotaged his planned move to a Catholic faculty after a spell abroad in a secular university. 'My wife and I had our bags packed,' he said. 'But we were suddenly informed that my appointment had been blocked by Rome, because of my alleged support for the ordination of women. I had never written on this subject, but the inference was drawn because I am married to a Protestant. Both the university authorities and the local bishop had ratified my appointment. They were as shocked and angered as I was. No one in Ratzinger's office would talk directly to me. My letters went unanswered. Every piece of news came my way through third parties.'

* * *

The investigation of Charles Curran is in some ways the most significant piece of CDF business in recent decades, because he

67

has persistently linked discussion of sexual ethics to underlying questions about authority and the legitimacy of public dissent. Even before *Humanae Vitae*, Curran had made a name for himself as an independent voice, and published many articles arguing that forbidden activities such as masturbation, contraception and pre-marital sex were not necessarily sinful. Known for intellectual rigour as well as courtesy, he has always maintained that his arguments have solid theological foundations. In the matter of family planning, for example, he claims a biblical warrant for his view that sex has a psychological aspect apart from procreation. Some conservatives portray this debate as a clash between loyal devotees of the tradition and relativists who have capitulated to secular fashion. Curran recasts the terms of the discussion. He argues that contraception is a second-order issue on which there can be principled disagreement between sincere and well-informed Christians – just as, for example, over pacifism and the use of force.

His difficulties began in 1967, when he was told that his contract in the theology faculty at the Catholic University of America in Washington, DC, was being ended. It appeared that the bishops and cardinals among the university's trustees had faced pressure from the CDF to act against him. But Curran's colleagues voted to strike unless he was reinstated, and the student body supported this decision. The authorities gave way, and Curran got his job back. Never a faint heart, he used the publication of *Humanae Vitae* in July of the following year to repeat his arguments in favour of birth control. A statement drawn up with colleagues (and later signed by more than six hundred other scholars) declared that 'spouses may responsibly decide according to their conscience that artificial contraception in some circumstances is permissible and indeed necessary to . . . foster the values . . . of marriage.'

This argument was also expressed in a declaration by Bernhard Häring, widely viewed as one of the most distinguished moralists in the Catholic world at this time:

> Whoever can be convinced that the absolute forbidding of artificial means of birth control as stated by *Humanae Vitae* is the correct interpretation of divine law must earnestly endeavour to live according to this conviction. Whoever, however, after serious reflection and prayer is convinced that

in his or her case a prohibition could not be the will of God, should in inner peace follow his/her conscience and not thereby feel her/himself to be a second-class Catholic.[4]

A second attempt to sack Curran (this time spearheaded by the Archbishop of Los Angeles, Cardinal James McIntyre) was set in motion, but he was again vindicated after an inquiry by the university's board of trustees. Curran assumed that his argument about the possibility of legitimate dissent was now broadly accepted, especially after bishops in Germany and elsewhere also stated that birth control was a matter of conscience, and the American bishops issued a document, *Human Life in Our Day*, which acknowledged the acceptability of dissent on three conditions: that the rationale is serious, and that the form of dissent does not assail the Church's teaching authority, nor constitute a source of scandal. The meaning here was vague – and, in the eyes of conservatives, question-begging. But the essential point, for Curran, is that the *principle* of valid dissent had been conceded. In a correspondence with Vatican officials extending over many years, he could never induce them to accept this principle, and concluded that Rome had effectively repudiated *Human Life in Our Day* without admitting it.

Curran's battle with Ratzinger has been rehearsed elsewhere,[5] and it would be superfluous to reproduce it here in detail. The main features of the case are as follows. Proceedings against Curran were launched by the CDF at some point during the 1970s, and in 1979, he responded to observations on his work with five questions of his own. Among other things, he asked whether a theologian had the right to express public dissent from the teaching of the so-called ordinary magisterium (the official but non-infallible corpus of church teaching) and whether the ordinary magisterium was the only component in the teaching role of the Church. He also enquired whether the teaching of the ordinary magisterium had not been mistaken at various times in the past, and whether dissident theologians had not played a central part in correcting earlier errors. (He had in mind such subjects as the temporal power of the Church; slavery, which was accepted as a fact of life by the Vatican until the 1860s; the burning of witches; and the condemnation of the *nouvelle théologie* during the 1950s – an episode that saw Ratzinger himself on the rebel side.)

For the CDF, however, the fact of Curran's dissent was enough, especially as he held a position in a Catholic university. Ratzinger, after an initial exchange of correspondence at the outset of his time as Prefect, wrote at greater length to Curran in 1983, arguing that personal dissent from the teaching of the ordinary magisterium was not synonymous with a right to public dissent, and accusing him of treating the position of the magisterium as he would 'the opinion of an ordinary theologian'. The following year, he put the point even more strongly: 'To dissent even privately requires personal certitude that the teaching of the Church is incorrect. To further dissent publicly and to encourage dissent in others runs the risk of causing scandal to the faithful . . .' Curran stood by his central assertion in an answer to Ratzinger written in June 1983. He doubted that real dialogue could continue unless the Congregation stated whether or not it accepted 'any possibility of legitimate public theological dissent in the Church'. Far from accepting that principled dissent was a source of scandal, he went on, he found it more offensive to cloak the truth. In this letter and subsequently, Curran also addressed the headline issues, including masturbation and pre-marital sex.

In the autumn of 1985, Ratzinger replied that anyone subscribing to such views could not be considered a Catholic theologian. Curran's *missio canonica* would be withdrawn unless he recanted. There was no subsequent meeting of minds between the two, despite a face-to-face encounter at the CDF offices in March 1986 at which the accused was supported by a pack of moral theologians including Häring, and a compromise plan under which Curran's 'errors' would be enumerated, and he would stop teaching sexual ethics. Curran refused to back down, and was accordingly stripped of his right to teach shortly after. This led to the loss of his job at the Catholic University of America. He remains a priest in good standing, and now holds a chair at Southern Methodist University in Texas.

* * *

As we have seen, the Vatican has been prepared to condemn what it holds to be corrupt forms of heterosexual activity, but gay sex has formed an especially important touchstone of discussion on the limits of diversity. An early sign of Ratzinger's attitudes came in 1983, when he sought to stop publication of *A Challenge to*

Love: Gay and Lesbian Catholics in the Church,[6] a collection edited
by Fr Robert Nugent. Nugent, a member of the Society of the
Divine Saviour, and his friend Sr Jeannine Gramick, of the School
Sisters of Notre Dame, are pioneers of ministry to homosexuals
in the United States, and have often been reserved about their
attitude to official teaching. Ratzinger succeeded merely in forcing
Bishop Walter Sullivan of Richmond, Virginia, to excise his name
from the book, but the broader campaign againt Nugent and
Gramick was only deferred. At the same time, Archbishop
Raymond Hunthausen of Seattle allowed the gay Catholic group
Dignity to hold a Mass in his cathedral celebrated by Fr John
McNeill, a Jesuit subsequently expelled from his order for backing
changes to official teaching. Three years later, in 1986, many of
Hunthausen's powers were transferred to his auxiliary bishop,
but they were restored shortly afterwards.

A more significant development in 1986 was the publication of
a CDF statement, *Homosexualitatis Problema,* addressed to all
Catholic bishops. This described the homosexual inclination as 'a
more or less strong tendency towards an intrinsic moral evil'. The
document also contains a warning to pastors that 'No authentic
pastoral programme will include organisations in which homosexual persons associate with each other without clearly stating
that homosexual activity is immoral', and expresses misgivings
about growing toleration of gay lifestyles. Homosexuality is said
to have 'a direct impact on society's understanding of the nature
and rights of the family and puts them in jeopardy'.

Homosexualitatis Problema was widely described as a figleaf for
prejudice by secular commentators, especially as Ratzinger always
refused to meet gay Catholic representatives, both then and later.
The Cardinal viewed the criticism as inherently misplaced. Human
rights, according to his reading of Christian tradition, always
derive from right actions. On this view, there could be no right to
overthrow the law of nature. But Ratzinger's sharpest critics
challenged him on his own ground. In the first place, they said, it
would be very inaccurate to characterise debates on sexuality, no
less than on birth control, as a clash between the ungodly and the
forces of light. Many liberal Catholics believe that biblical
pronouncements on homosexuality (and, for that matter, on
subjects including cosmology, borrowing with interest, polygamy,
eternal hellfire, and the need to stone disobedient children) are
simply mistaken, and part of a superseded cultural milieu. Others,

though, have posed a subtler question, namely how solid the so-called biblical case against same-sex relations really is. Old Testament scholars now mostly agree that the destruction of Sodom and Gommorah in Genesis 19 is a consequence of rape and the flouting of rules of hospitality, rather than homosexuality as such; while the prohibition of same-sex activity in Leviticus forms part of a legal code that Christians hold to have been supplanted by the New Covenant. (Christ's followers do not observe Old Testament dietary requirements, among other laws.) Paul's condemnation of libertinism in Romans 1 has also been seized on by those who favour a relaxation of church teaching, because this and other relevant scriptural passages presuppose that all are heterosexual, and only engage in gay sex through wilful perversity. This, say reformers, is plainly false. The Bible may well be right in condemning heterosexuals involved in same-sex activity for gratification, but it has no line on stable, monogamous partnerships. And since Scripture in its totality lays much emphasis on the role of physical love in bonding, as well as breeding, then there is a theological rationale for gay relationships analogous to the case for contraception.

These arguments may not be the last word on the subject of Christianity and homosexuality, but they are a long way from reflecting the wantonness with which the CDF charges dissenters. On the contrary, the attempt to read Scripture with more attention to textual and historical nuance is precisely a mark of the *ressourcement* approach applied to such effect by Ratzinger in other spheres. No such awareness is apparent in *Homosexualitis Problema*, which has set the tone for all official statements on the gay issue subsequently. In late 1987, the United States Bishops' Conference published a report, *The Many Faces of Aids: a Global Response*, arguing that condoms might be used in some circumstances to impede the spread of HIV infection. In January 1988, Ratzinger was assailed by pro-gay demonstrators at St Peter's Lutheran Church in New York City, some of whom screamed 'Heil Hitler' and 'Inquisitor' at him. Several arrests were made, after which the Cardinal resumed his address in a calm manner, which drew enthusiastic applause from many who remained in the audience. Four months later, however, he rejected the bishops' pro-condom argument in a letter relayed by the papal nuncio, and used the row as grounds for clamping down on the American hierarchy more generally. When statements were made on contentious issues, advance consultation with the Holy See was advisable, he warned.

Conscious that the United States was the main source of the gay rights movement, CDF officials maintained their pressure on the American bishops during the years that followed. In 1992, for example, Ratzinger publicly urged them to resist legislation permitting gay unions, or giving same-sex couples the right to adopt children, and again defended the propriety of anti-gay discrimination: 'there are areas in which it is not unjust discrimination to take sexual orientation into account, for example, in employment of teachers or coaches, and in military recruitment . . . The passage from the recognition of homosexuality as a factor on which basis it is illegal to discriminate can easily lead, if not automatically, to the legislative protection of homosexuality.' And in 1998, bishops' conferences everywhere were muzzled by *Apostolos Suos*, a Vatican document declaring that these bodies could not make statements on faith or morals that were not agreed unanimously or issued with Rome's prior approval.

During the 1990s, attitudes to gay ministry became steadily more symptomatic of tension between liberal and conservative church leaders in America. Progressive voices, though accepting the official teaching that gay sex could never be approved, sought nevertheless to make pastoral provision for celibate gay Catholics and their families. As reported, Nugent and Gramick were in the forefront of such work; and by 1999, Ratzinger had resolved to stop them in their tracks. In May of that year, after trying and failing to have them sign a document affirming that homosexual acts 'are always objectively evil', he permanently banned them from ministry to lesbians and gay men. 'It was clear', said the Cardinal, 'that the activities of Sister Gramick and Father Nugent were causing difficulties in not a few dioceses and that they were continuing to present the teaching of the Church as one possible option among others and as open to fundamental change.'

The accused pair reiterated their willingness to affirm the 'core beliefs' of Catholicism, but insisted on the right of every believer to maintain the privacy of their conscience 'in matters which are not central to our faith'. The CDF was still not satisfied. A year later, Nugent and Gramick were called to Rome and told by the heads of their respective orders that they were banned not only from speaking or writing about homosexuality, but also from making any comment on the sanctions they had incurred. Gramick

73

has left the School Sisters of Notre Dame, but now belongs to another community, the Loreto Sisters. Nugent remains in his order, and spent a year in 2004–05 on sabbatical in London. His work is now more parish-based, but he is reasonably sanguine about the prospects for gay ministry generally. 'My impression is that people are often just getting on with their lives without a lot of fuss,' he told me.

The apparent novelty of Ratzinger's actions in this case were spelt out in an article for the Jesuit magazine *America* by Lisa Sowle Cahill, a professor at Boston College:

> While one might argue that the fullness of Catholic teaching includes points pastorally downplayed by Nugent and Gramick (the intrinsic evil and immorality of homosexual acts), Vatican policy on conformity and dissent has certainly taken a novel turn by focusing on this fact. Now the bottom line of orthodoxy is full disclosure of church teaching on an issue, rather than the avoidance of any claims that contradict it.[7]

Sowle Cahill then pointed to a double standard evident in the selective application of this maximalist criterion. If the CDF were to be consistent, she suggested, then every defender of the just war would have to make an equally clear declaration 'that violence violates Christian identity', and every defender of capitalism should state that globalisation sometimes harms the rights of the poor.

*   *   *

A similar picture has applied with Ratzinger's opposition to the ordination of women. The proposed reform is rejected not just as inconsistent with tradition, but as an assault on sexual complementarity, and, by implication, a form of blasphemy. Ratzinger elaborates this second, drastic argument in a book-length interview with Peter Seewald, a German journalist, entitled *Salt of the Earth*:

> The idea that 'nature' has something to say is no longer admissible; man is to have the liberty to remodel himself at will. He is to be free from all of the prior givens of his essence. He makes of himself what he wants, and only in this way is he really

'free and liberated'. Behind this approach is a rebellion on man's part against the limits that he has as a biological being. In the end, it is a revolt against our creatureliness. Man is to be his own creator – a modern, new edition of the immemorial attempt to be God, to be like God.[8]

This comment represents a considerable intensification of a claim first spelt out formally during the post-conciliar period in *Inter Insigniores*, known in English as 'On the Admission of Women to the Priesthood', published by the CDF in 1976. Its pitch, familiar through many repetitions during the past three decades, is that because Jesus chose only male apostles, his intention must have been deliberate and binding. The Church therefore has no power to alter a practice instituted by the Lord. Yet there were many previous cases in which the Church had declared a reform to be inopportune, only to change its mind later on. In the eyes of some, the women-priests issue fell into such a category, as it dealt with current discipline rather than revelation. It was to rule out just this sort of reasoning that the relevant canon was restated in even stronger terms by John Paul II in his 1994 apostolic letter, *Ordinatio Sacerdotalis*, 'On the Reserving of Priestly Ordination to Men Alone'. In order 'that all doubt may be removed regarding a matter of great importance,' he wrote, 'I declare that the Church has no authority whatsoever to confer priestly ordination on women, and that this judgement is to be definitively held by all the Church's faithful.'

In 1995, a query arose whether this teaching could be described as infallible, and Ratzinger's answer, in a brief CDF statement, was 'yes'. The logically tidy-minded then asked whether Ratzinger's statement was itself infallible. Questioned later on the matter, he gave the following rationale for his view:

the answer, confirmed by the Pope, that we, the Congregation for the Doctrine of the Faith, gave to the issue of women's ordination does not say that the Pope has now performed an infallible act of teaching. The Pope rather established that the Church, the bishops of all places and times, have always taught and acted in this way. The Second Vatican Council says: What bishops teach and do in unison over a very long time is infallible; it is the expression of a bond that they themselves did not create.[9]

Behind this comment (and of much more than academic interest alone) lies a distinction between three kinds of truth recognised in canon 833 of the Code of Canon Law. There are truths which are divinely revealed. They are taught with the highest level of authority as dogmas of faith. Then there are truths which are not in themselves revealed, but are so necessarily connected with the faith that the Church can speak in a definitive way about them in order to defend or explain some aspect of revelation. Catholics are required 'firmly to accept and hold' such truths, but not with an assent of faith in the proper sense of the term. Third, the Code identifies the kind of teaching that one finds in papal encyclicals, and Vatican documents produced with papal approval. These demand 'submission of will and intellect', which the American theologian Francis Sullivan glosses as 'an attitude of willingness to accept such teaching and to form one's judgement on matters of faith and morals in accordance with it, as far as one is able'.[10]

The core point here is that Ratzinger realised the ban on women's ordination cannot belong to the first of these three categories. In an important CDF document published in 1990, the 'Instruction on the Ecclesial Vocation of the Theologian', he writes that 'When the magisterium proposes "in a definitive way" truths concerning faith and morals, which, even if not divinely revealed, are nevertheless strictly and intimately connected with Revelation, these must be firmly accepted and held.' In other words, Sullivan explains,

> this paragraph speaks of truths which are not dogmas calling for the assent of faith. When the Church has made a 'definitive' statement on some issue by reason of its necessary connection with Revelation, the faithful are called upon to accept and hold that statement as true. It is official Catholic doctrine, though not a dogma of faith, that when the Church makes a truly definitive statement on such a matter, it teaches with infallibility. Even if it is certain that the magisterium has spoken infallibly, however, its statement does not become a dogma calling for the assent of faith, since this is only given to revealed truth.

Sullivan draws a very important inference from this: even if it were clearly established that the Church had infallibly taught something that, while pertaining to the deposit of faith, was not actually contained in it, its statement would not be a dogma calling for the assent of faith, nor would one be guilty of heresy for denying it. Sullivan does not say so, but it is this point, in the view of reformers, which feeds the hope that the Catholic Church may eventually sanction the ordination of women, despite a hardline reavowal of official teaching in the 1998 apostolic letter *Ad Tuendam Fidem* ('For the Defence of the Faith').

Ratzinger has adduced two further theological arguments in support of his position. First, he suggests that the all-male tradition of Christian priesthood cannot be a social convention alone, because many ancient religious systems employed priestesses. The Church could have followed suit, but deliberately did not do so. Second, he refers to an argument associated with Elisabeth Schüssler-Fiorenza, a pioneer of feminist theology in Germany and the United States. This expresses unease with priesthood as such, because of the link between ordination and subordination.[11] Ratzinger sees a critical weakness in reformers' arguments here. They misconstrue the debate as a matter of power and equality. Priesthood, properly understood, is a ministry of service.

Again, many Catholic theologians have been unpersuaded by what they view as a mixture of unsubstantiated assertion and straw-man tactics. Certainly, there are bad arguments in favour of women priests, and a newer generation of Catholic feminists is critical of a tendency among the pioneers to swallow secular ideas without discrimination. They have been as happy as Ratzinger to shun inappropriate models of priesthood, and to emphasise that sin is a universal category, not (as some feminists have implied) applicable to the male sex alone. But this is a sideshow for other supporters of women priests who maintain that it is logically wrong to think that an argument is invalid simply because it can be supported by sloppy arguments.

Rehearsed ad nauseam elsewhere, their case rests on the proposition that Christ assumed representative humanity, not only maleness, at the incarnation, so that neither the gender – nor, for that matter, the Jewishness – of the apostles are essential constituents of priesthood. The New Testament, in any case, says nothing about *ministerial* priests, and arguments from silence or near-silence may therefore be considered dubious. Some (especially Anglican) theologians go further, arguing that the full extent of priestly symbolism can be appreciated *only* in a setting in which women as well as men can stand at the altar *in persona Christi*. These, too, are substantial arguments; yet they have not been seriously assessed in the publications of the CDF. *Ordinatio Sacerdotalis* has a sting in the tail. It says that Catholics are no longer at liberty to discuss the subject of women priests. Even some supporters of the status quo were taken aback by the peremptoriness of this edict.

*　　*　　*

More than any subject in which Ratzinger became involved as Prefect, the dispute over liberation theology evokes images of scarlet-clad prelates harassing servants of the poor from the splendour of marble halls in Rome. That such a portrayal does not belong wholly to the province of fantasy is demonstrated by the obstacles put in the way of some clergy guilty of nothing more than living out the gospel. But it needs heavy qualification with reference to Ratzinger's own account of what he was seeking to do. Those who deplore the oversimplifications evident in his teaching on sexual ethics owe it to him to consider the cartoonish images of his political thought with care. Doing so is not a matter of courtesy alone. Liberation theology is not one system, and its seeds have fallen on many kinds of soil.

First, there is the element focused on listening, and responding to the needs of the disadvantaged. This emerged strongly at the meeting of CELAM, the umbrella body for Latin America's bishops, at the Columbian city of Medellín in 1968. It produced ground-breaking statements on the option for the poor, and an allied sense that the Church had for too long kept silent in the face of chronic injustice. Archbishop Hélder Câmara of Recife in Brazil, a hero of this style, is often remembered for a celebrated soundbite: 'When I give food to the poor, they call me a saint; when I ask why the poor have no food, they call me a Communist.' Archbishop Oscar Romero of San Salvador, whom one would not call a classic liberation theologian, was also converted in a simple way to listening to the poor, and was murdered in 1980 by a right-wing death squad for his pains. The values of these leaders survive in at least some of the so-called base communities that sprung up around the continent during the 1970s and 80s.

The opponents are almost as diverse as the movement itself. Some critics have expressed unease with liberation theology on purely economic grounds. They argue that it has been severely mistaken in seeing capitalism as the great enemy, when a capitalist tradition is precisely what Latin America has generally lacked. Until the late twentieth century, large parts of the continent were conquistador societies in which almost all wealth was concentrated in the hands of a privileged few. According to this argument, if only capitalism had taken root at an early stage, then prosperity, stable institutions and a sizeable middle class would have developed in its wake. Nothing dates so quickly as attempts to keep up with current fashions, and the readiness of some Christian thinkers to express themselves in Marxist terms now appears rash.

At a more conceptual level, an often repeated criticism is that the movement itself tends to be the property of a foreign-educated élite. For all their talk about the people, many liberation theologians' inspiration is European. Strongly influenced by Karl Rahner and the Rahnerian style, they have a strongly positive understanding of human nature, which forms a stepping stone to a more thoroughgoing endorsement of Marxist or marxisant arguments. Other liberationists show a debt to the Frankfurt school of Marxism, famous for its apocalyptic element. This includes the belief that saving conflagrations are possible – that, on the far side of an intensified conflict, it will be possible for human beings to be really human. It's a potent myth, and has just enough in common with Christian vocabulary for the two models to be yoked together in some circumstances. The difficulties come in three areas. First, armed conflict, where different liberation theologians have taken very different approaches. Christianity does not sanction revolutionary violence; and this is a historical fact that sits very uneasily with some Marxist language. Second, there is a question about revelation. Does Christianity simply confirm a programme that is already emerging under its own steam? A third query concerns the characteristically Marxist theme of false consciousness. Should the liberation theologian say that the task of listening to the people needs to be balanced by a critical exposé of ways in which popular consciousness feeds a delusive and oppressive reality?

This is the background against which Ratzinger's policies can be explained and, in his supporters' eyes, defended. His first major statement on the subject, *Libertatis Nuntius* ('Instruction on Certain Aspects of the "Theology of Liberation"'), was issued in

September 1984. Summing up its contents soon afterwards, he said that in Europe, liberation theology

> is generally identified simply with commitment to the poor, and every criticism is interpreted as an attack on action on behalf of the poor. The aggressive passion, which also surfaces in people who do not themselves scorn the comforts of European affluence, is a problem of its own kind. The radical representatives of liberation theology regard criticism as an expression of class interest: he who voices it ranges himself on the side of the oppressors and wants to cement the current power structure. Where the scheme of class warfare becomes the only key for understanding reality and thought patterns, criticism and fruitful dialogue are made impossible. Furthermore, any social reform and non-revolutionary action on behalf of the poor comes under suspicion as a means of maintaining the power which stabilises the system. Revolution becomes repudiation of reform and of direct action as performed, for instance, by Mother Teresa.[12]

He also complains that some liberationists 'do not seem to see the real and practical problems of how a society is to be organised after the Revolution'. The Cardinal goes on to say that he is 'painfully moved by this hardly Christian dream of creating the new man not by requiring conversion of the individual but as it were from the outside, simply by changing the conditions of production'.[13]

Signs of an impending crackdown were visible at various stages in the year before *Libertatis Nuntius*, including the 1979 CELAM meeting at Puebla in Mexico, at which John Paul II distinguished between 'Christian' and 'ideological' forms of liberation; the plans by Vatican officials (including Ratzinger's predecessor as Prefect, Cardinal Franjo Seper) to reassign Archbishop Romero before his assassination in 1980; and Ratzinger's demand that the Peruvian bishops investigate Gustavo Gutiérrez in 1983. The charge sheet focused on an allegedly Marxist conception of history, and an unorthodox doctrine of the Church.

The CDF moved directly against Boff during the following year. Though not in the same intellectual league theologically as Gutiérrez or another major figure such as Jon Sobrino, he was to become a figurehead in the battle over liberation theology for two main reasons: his nationality and his ecclesiology. A summons to Rome arrived in May 1984, along with a statement requesting clarification of his book later published in English as *Church: Charism and Power*.[14] Ratzinger accused Boff of suggesting that the structure of the Catholic Church was not divinely authorised, and of having a free-floating doctrine of the Holy Spirit.

Libertatis Nuntius caused a flurry of discussion, much of it heated. The Vatican Secretary of State, Cardinal Casaroli (the only curial official with equivalent clout to Ratzinger), complained that he had not been consulted, and that the document displayed a negative tone. Others observed that the Instruction seemed mealy-mouthed about Christian commitment to the poor, and that it took a far less measured line on liberation theology than an ITC paper on the subject produced seven years earlier. Juan Luis Segundo, one of the best-known liberation theologians after Gutiérrez, argued that Ratzinger was betraying the spirit of *Gaudium et Spes*. There were even suggestions that John Paul – who appeared to blow hot and cold about liberation theology generally – was also uneasy about the Instruction, and wanted it balanced by other material. (Two years later, he himself would say in a letter to the Brazilian bishops that liberation theology was 'not only opportune, but useful and necessary'.)

Whether these indicators are reliable or, as is more likely, John Paul's underlying view was a softer version of Ratzinger's, the CDF line was to triumph in stages over the years that followed. On 11 March 1985, *Church: Charism and Power* was condemned in Rome, and several weeks later, Boff was told that he could not speak, teach or publish for an indefinite period. This sanction was lifted within two years, but further restrictions were imposed on him subsequently, culminating in a demand that he step down as editor of the magazine *Vozes* in 1991. He left the priesthood shortly afterwards, and later married his secretary, with whom he had begun a relationship long before resigning his orders.

The CDF position was restated in purely theological terms in a second document, *Libertatis Conscientia* ('Instruction on Christian Freedom and Liberation'), issued in 1986. A decisive sign that events were turning the conservatives' way emerged in 1992, at the fourth CELAM conference, held in Santo Domingo under the chairmanship of Jorge Medina (Ratzinger's old *Communio* ally) and Casaroli's successor, Cardinal Angelo Sodano. This gathering upheld the substance of the CDF instructions, and some observers date the gradual eclipse of liberation theology from this point.

If we recall Timothy Radcliffe's remark quoted at the outset of this chapter, then it seems fair to infer that at least some of the questions raised about Boff were valid. (Several theologians interviewed off the record for this book described his ecclesiology as Protestant in all but name.) But there are also grounds for thinking that Ratzinger's policies have done considerable damage. This book cannot provide more than a snapshot of a continent-wide situation, but the example of Hélder Câmara was not out of the ordinary. This saintly man (who served in Recife from 1964 to 1985) was no ideologue. He was simply among the first generation of clerics to reorder local church structures as a mark of concern for the poor. The governance of his diocese became more transparent through a series of consultative bodies, one of which was a pastoral assembly including laypeople from many walks of life; and a justice and peace commission was established to support political prisoners under the country's military dictatorship. Help was also given to groups threatened with eviction by landowners or speculators. The core of Câmara's strategy was the network of base communities that met for action and study even in the poorest areas. The diocesan seminary was replaced by 15 small households, each based in a disadvantaged parish. Dom Helder also established the Recife Theological Institute, open to anyone who wanted to study. He made clear in his inaugural lecture how unlike comparable colleges this would be. Its intake, he declared, could include 'agnostics and atheists, very often Christians in practice'.

Câmara was saluted by John Paul as 'brother of the poor, my brother', in 1980, but his reforms were swiftly undone by his successor as Archbishop, Jose Cardoso, a canon lawyer with scarcely any pastoral experience. Francis McDonagh, a development worker and journalist with long experience of South America, now gives a gloomy prognosis:

> The model of the Church that has been dismantled so violently in Recife was, it now seems clear, the very model that had begun to emerge at [Vatican II] in its idea of the Church as the 'people of God' – a term seldom found in Vatican texts these days. It was a model in which lay women and men bring their experience to bear on the Church's ministry, theology and liturgy as of right; and the roles of clergy and laity are redefined in the light of the community's needs.[15]

* * *

A final illustration relevant to this overview is that of Jacques Dupuis. This case also provoked many complaints that Ratzinger was a player as well as a referee, and that his office sometimes displayed excessive zeal. Look no further than the official texts, analysts often suggest – especially *Dominus Iesus*, issued in 2000 – and the changing atmosphere during John Paul II's pontificate is plain to see. *Nostra Aetate*, Vatican II's declaration on interfaith relations, announced that 'The Catholic Church rejects nothing which is true and holy in [other] religions. She has a sincere respect for those ways of acting and living, those moral and doctrinal teachings which may differ in many respects from what she holds and teaches, but which none the less often reflect the brightness of that Truth which is the light of men.'

As Terrence Merrigan has explained in an illuminating article about Dupuis, his theology of religions is propelled by a typically Catholic interest in how God's saving presence is mediated to the world. Since the Second Vatican Council sees this presence as universal, Dupuis was concerned to pose more precisely the question of how it operates. It has been common to identify three broad schools of thought on interfaith dialogue: exclusivism, inclusivism and pluralism. Exclusivists take a dim view of non-Christian traditions. Pluralists believe that other faiths can offer paths to God on an equal footing with Christianity, and are therefore frequently opposed in principle to missionary activity. Inclusivists are a more varied group, but mostly endorse some variation of the belief that other faiths may provide de facto scope for salvation. This spectrum in turn reflects a perhaps inevitable instability in church teaching. Paradoxically, for example, John 14:6 ('I am the way, and the truth, and the life. No one comes to the Father, but by me') is not only used as a proof text by conservatives. For Christians favouring a more welcoming attitude to other faiths, the true meaning of this verse is that no one comes to the Father except by the Word – God's reason and wisdom which (as John's Prologue discloses) enlightens the hearts of all humanity.

Dupuis – a professor at the Gregorian University in Rome, who died in 2001, after prolonged illness – did not regard other religions as being on an equal footing with Christianity in the divine scheme of salvation. In his eyes, their value rests on a participation in the saving work of Christ. His theories are set out in the book that led to CDF action against him, *Toward A Christian Theology of Religious Pluralism*. But as Merrigan explains, he also went beyond the traditional position by investing non-Christian religions 'with a real mediatory role on behalf of their members', and claimed inspiration from John Paul II, who also thought that 'participated mediation' in the work of Christ was to be found outside the Church. 'In highlighting the positive role that these religions play in the economy of salvation,' Merrigan continues:

> Dupuis is adopting a position reminiscent of the so-called pluralist theology of religions. Indeed, he describes his own position as an 'inclusive pluralism'. [But for] the pluralists, the many religions represent independently valid paths to salvation. There is no necessary link to Jesus Christ. Dupuis resolutely refuses this view of things, and defends the position that Christ is always implicated in the event of salvation.[16]

Merrigan's conclusion is that Dupuis is best regarded as a pioneer at the cutting edge of the Catholic theology of religions, a theologian intent on extending Catholic thought in order to do justice to our contemporary pluralistic context. 'It is not surprising that his research opens up untried paths which may or may not be dead ends.'

Dominus Iesus ('On the Unicity [*sic*] and Salvific Universality of Jesus Christ and the Church'), however, takes a much harder line, both in substance and tone. It denounces relativism and religious pluralism, and describes non-Christians and even non-Roman Catholics as being 'in a gravely deficient situation' compared with 'those who, in the Church, have the fullness of the means of salvation'. This document came hard on the heals of a brief CDF declaration, 'Note on the Expression "Sister Churches"', which ruled that this term could be applied only to the Orthodox Churches, but not to the Anglicans, or other Reformed traditions. Many commentators were dismayed, sensing that the ecumenical progress of the previous three decades was in jeopardy.

Dupuis remained uncertain about *Dominus Iesus*. He thought that it was right to reject defences of *de jure* religious pluralism that deny the uniqueness of Christ as universal saviour. But in a public lecture he argued that the document was wrong in seeming to imply that any theological theory supporting religious pluralism in principle must be based on the denial of what is in fact the very core of Christian faith. There is no lack of theologians today who seek to combine and hold together, even if in a fruitful tension, their unimpaired faith in Jesus Christ as universal saviour of mankind, on the one hand, and, on the other, a positive, salvific significance of the other religious traditions for their followers, in accordance with the eternal plan of God for humanity.[17]

Dupuis first learnt of CDF action against him in 1998. He was informed that *Toward a Christian Theology of Religious Pluralism* was suspected of containing errors against the faith. Two years of anxiety and ill health (he had long suffered from a severe kidney ailment) followed before he was given the chance to meet CDF officials; a hearing attended by Ratzinger took place in September 2000. The accused was supported by his fellow Jesuit and former colleague Gerald O'Collins, who is in no doubt that the case for the prosecution lacked substance. 'In the end,' O'Collins reports, 'a Notification was issued in February 2001 in which the subject of errors against the faith was not mentioned. It merely said that *Toward a Christian Theology of Religious Pluralism* was open to misinterpretation. You could say that about the Bible, too! The CDF charge sheet had not included page references; so it was hard for me to refute their arguments one by one; but I emphasised the many occasions on which the book described Jesus as the constitutive saviour of all men and women.' O'Collins also points out the link between his friend's arguments and traditional teaching on the incarnation. 'Dupuis stressed that the divine operations of Christ transcend his human operations. There is no separation, but there is a distinction. The divine operations of the Logos are therefore not limited by the incarnation and resurrection.'

It is hard to overstate the broader implication of this argument. Dupuis, no less than his 'orthodox' critics, felt that he had been faithful to the spirit of the gospel, and that his arguments dovetailed with fundamental planks of the faith. Ratzinger's reaction, and his arguments in *Dominus Iesus*, also need to be understood in terms of underlying convictions. In a rare example of a difference of view with John Paul II, he jibbed when the Pope invited a group of interfaith leaders to pray for peace with him at

Assisi in 1986. The venture was not repeated. In particular, the Prefect disliked the open-handed attitude of *Nostra Aetate* – a document very similar in spirit to *Gaudium et Spes*. He was determined to lay a firm hand on the Church's tiller in consequence.

6

Controversialist and Apologist

If as Prefect, Ratzinger let his principles inform his agenda so markedly, then a more detailed excursus is needed to shed light on his cast of mind. A vivid sample of his sombre outlook comes in *Rapporto sulla fede* (published in English as *The Ratzinger Report* in 1985[1]), which was based on conversations with Vittorio Messori, an Italian journalist. For a view of Ratzinger's sunnier side, we can look at *Salt of the Earth* and another volume originating in interviews with Peter Seewald: *God and the World*.[2] Many *Vaticanisti* were taken aback by the provenance of these later books. Seewald was a lapsed Catholic when he met the Cardinal in 1996 to record *Salt of the Earth*, and remained uncommitted four years later during the encounter that produced *God and the World*. Many of his questions are to the point; others display an unfamiliarity with theology and church affairs. Some are acerbic. But Ratzinger speaks with assurance, showing himself as a very able Christian apologist. The experience helped Seewald recover his faith.[3]

Messori's interview appeared in an abridged form in the *Deutsche Tagenpost*, a German Catholic newspaper, in December 1984. *Rapporto sulla fede* appeared several months later. Ratzinger's downbeat tone on the subject of post-Vatican II Catholicism rarely falters. 'Certainly the development since the Council seems to be cruelly in contradiction with expectations, beginning with those of John XXIII and then of Paul VI and the majority of the Council Fathers' he says.

> A new Catholic unity had been hoped for. Instead, a dissent has divided us which, in the words of [Pope Paul], has gone from self-criticism to self-destruction. A new enthusiasm had been expected . . . [In its place] we are confronted with a process of

manifold collapse, which has developed to a great extent under the aegis of appealing to the Council, and thus has discredited it in many peoples' eyes. So the balance seems negative, and I repeat here what I said ten years after the end of the Council: it is impossible to contest that this period, in large parts of the world, has been remarkably unfavorable for the Catholic Church.

'To my mind,' he continues, 'the Council cannot really be made responsible for developments which stand in opposition both to the spirit and the letter of its documents. What is true is that, during the Council and in contradiction to its intentions, the so-called "Spirit of the Council" was born, which was and is really an anti-spirit, an incubus.' Then comes the Cardinal's most widely quoted remark:

> I have the impression that the misfortunes that the Church has encountered in the last twenty years are to be ascribed less to the 'true' Council than . . . to the fact that latently present polemical and centrifugal forces have [generated] a cultural crisis in the West, where the affluent middle class, the new tertiary-educated bourgeoisie (*die obere Mittelschicht, das neue Tertiärbürgertum*), with its liberal-radical ideology of individualistic, rationalistic, hedonistic character, is placing Christian values fundamentally in question.[4]

Ratzinger progressively widens his focus. He describes the late 1960s in particular as a time when Catholics moved from a 'narrow, inward-fixed Christianity' to an 'uncritical' openness to the world. Vatican II had rightly inaugurated a revision of Church–world relations.

> But you know neither Church nor world if you think that they could meet without conflict or that they could even coincide. On the contrary: the Christian today more than ever has to be clear that he belongs to a minority and that he is in opposition to what appears good, obvious and logical to the 'spirit of the world', as the New Testament calls it. One of the most urgent tasks of the Christian is to recover the capacity for nonconformism . . .

The longstanding doctrine that all who follow 'the commandments dictated by... conscience' can really obtain salvation has been 'one-sidedly and improperly radicalised, helped by catch-phrases such as "anonymous Christianity",' he declares. Parallel with this, religions are said to be of equal worth, leading to a corresponding decline in missionary impetus.

The Cardinal goes on to enumerate apparent crises in several fundamental areas of theology. Writing on the incarnation is said to be marked by an 'Arian' tendency to downplay or even deny the divinity of Christ. Allied to this is a 'widespread tendency to begin school bibles and catechism not with the Creation but with saving history (Abraham, Moses)', thus bypassing the question of God the Creator.

> The emphasis is all on history. One preserves oneself from a confrontation with Being. Reduced to such an isolated Christology – perhaps even to the man Jesus – God is no longer God, and the God of the Bible and Creed is no longer visible ... Hence the doubts about the 'material' aspects of revelation such as Mary's virginity, Jesus' real and concrete resurrection, and the resurrection of the body promised for all at the last day of history.

Speaking of the Church itself, Ratzinger says that 'in the Catholic consciousness to a greater or lesser degree a certain concept has widely spread – one resembling the model of certain North American sects and "free churches" rather than the classical Protestant model. It is the concept of the Church as a merely human organization [which] its members are free to restructure according to the needs of the moment.' A climate of this kind erodes the belief that doctrine is a given, and the inseparable link between Bible and Church, he suggests.

Reviewing the situation in North America, Ratzinger sees 'a world where money and consumption appear to be the measure of everything, so that the values represented by Catholicism appear more then ever "scandalous". The Church's moral teaching is perceived (as in Europe) as an ancient, alien body, clashing not only with the concrete way of life habitually led, but also with the basic mode of thought.' It is 'difficult if not impossible' to present 'the Catholic ethic' as reasonable; it is too remote from everything 'regarded as normal and self-evident'. Thus 'ethical problems stand in the foreground of theological work in North America, which has taken the lead also over Europe in this area, while European theology still claims a certain lead in exegesis and dogmatics.' In this climate, moral theology sees itself as facing a difficult choice confronting either society or the magisterium. 'Many of the better-known moral theologians opt for the latter, submitting themselves to compromises with a new bourgeois ethic which not seldom brings men and women into conflict with themselves . . . and subjects them to new forms of slavery, while claiming to free them.'

Ratzinger accuses feminist and liberation theologians of transporting Christian proclamation into a secular key. He is also asked about the activities of bishops, and the sometimes cacophonous notes struck by episcopal conferences. He replies that openness to the world was a reasonable priority for the Church during the Council and its immediate aftermath. But after the 'crisis of 1968' it became clearer that bishops also had to be capable of taking a stand against the 'negative developing tendencies' of secular society, and of 'correcting them when possible'. Episcopal conferences pose a problem: they 'are not based on theological foundations, as is the office of the individual bishop, but on practical, functional considerations', the Cardinal argues. One of the 'paradoxical' results of Vatican II was that 'the formation of episcopal conferences threatened the bishop's responsibility for the diocese in which he, in communion with the Church, is shepherd and teacher of the faith.' Thus the position of the bishop has been weakened. Ratzinger is also unimpressed by the bland tone of committee-drafted documents: 'the scandal and the folly of the Cross are easily lost in well-intentioned human prudence. Today more than ever that "salt" and the power of that "leaven" are needed.'

* * *

The Ratzinger Report was greeted with a chorus of surprise and misgiving. Some critics said that it reminded them of the *Syllabus of Errors* (1864), Pius IX's scatter-gun denunciation of modernity. Among the critics were senior French churchmen. Bishop Joseph Rozier of Poitiers told the weekly *La Vie* in July 1985 that Ratzinger's views were harsh and hidebound. 'The Church's entire evolution since the Council is gone through with a fine toothcomb, and everywhere he sees nothing but drift and perversion,' Rozier said.[5] Bishop Georges Gilson of Le Mans described the book's contents as 'holiday chatter' (*propos de vacances*).[6] It was a pity, he suggested, that the Cardinal had not expressed some gladness alongside all the hurt and disquiet, and he criticised Ratzinger for not waiting until the Extraordinary Synod of Bishops, called to consider the Church's future direction, had made its collective deliberations several months later. It met in November 1985, and did indeed show signs of Ratzinger's influence. A shocked *Tablet* correspondent was left in little doubt as to which way the wind was blowing.

> There is all the differerence between celebrating Vatican II and then adding that there have been errors, and concentrating on the errors before adding that Vatican II is to be celebrated. The report of the synod takes the second course, and in its opening section reflects closely the views of the German-speaking language group of which Cardinal Ratzinger was a member. Of course errors have followed Vatican II, as they follow every council, but surely they have been in no way so serious as the errors which followed Vatican I.[7]

Between the first draft and the final version of the synod report, a more positive sentence was added on the initiative of Cardinal Godfried Danneels, Archbishop of Malines-Brussels. It reads: 'the theology of the Cross in no way excludes the theology of creation and incarnation, but, as is obvious, presupposes it.' Some observers remained disappointed, however. Among them was Walter Kasper, then a professor of theology at Tübingen, and later one of Ratzinger's most formidable Vatican critics. In a confidential paper sent to the German bishops before the synod, he wrote that the Church still had a long way to go towards realising the vision of Vatican II: 'on all levels of church life, collegiality ... and participation ... in the spirit of the council are desirable, indeed, necessary ... In this respect, not all the legitimate(!) [*sic*] expectations of the council have been fulfilled.'[8]

In Britain, *The Ratzinger Report* prompted a counterblast in the Dominican journal *New Blackfriars* from a distinguished group of Catholic scholars. A special number began with an open letter to the bishops of England and Wales from the Editor, Fr John Orme

Mills, and the chairman of the editorial board, Fr Timothy Radcliffe. It argued that

> we will remain humanly and theologically immature unless we discover how, as a Church, to explore areas of dissent and disagreement without fear. The truthfulness of the Church is threatened by opposite forms of infantilism, both that which identifies communion with the bishop of Rome with an unquestioning acceptance of every word that comes from the Vatican, and that which is unable to tolerate a single word of criticism or correction from the wider Church, and especially from the centre. Both are renunciations of that dialogue whereby the Spirit leads us into all truth.

There followed four substantial essays by Professors Nicholas Lash and Eamon Duffy of Cambridge University, Fr Fergus Kerr of Blackfriars, Oxford, and Fr John Mahoney, a former Principal of Heythrop College, London.

Kerr's essay, 'The Cardinal and post-conciliar Britain',[9] begins by putting Ratzinger's 'morbid' diagnosis in a broader context. For at least 150 years after the early nineteenth century, Kerr points out, and with only the odd exception, papal and Vatican documents had exuded a similar spirit of gloom. The Church that has the infallibility with which the Divine Redeemer willed that she should be endowed, in the words of Vatican I, 'is repeatedly and repetitiously pictured in Roman rhetoric as being about to collapse [in the face] of external pressure and internal corruption'. Kerr finds it amazing 'how easily, from a Roman vantage point, the Catholic Church displays these alarming symptoms of almost terminal disease'.

He is no less surprised by the content of Ratzinger's arguments, describing them as 'remarkably academic and arcane', and perhaps reflecting 'the wounds of some internecine German professorial fracas'. For the average Irish or British Catholic, he continues, the recent past has been marked less by self-destructive dissent than by a welcome discovery of Catholic social teaching; yet rising concern for justice, peace and related issues is overlooked in Ratzinger's 'very lopsided' presentation. Kerr also takes issue with the Prefect's specifically doctrinal gripes. 'When someone in Cardinal Ratzinger's position holds forth on the "crisis of faith" in the Catholic Church he really needs to be extremely careful not to project an oratorical fantasy populated with straw-men and bugaboos,' Kerr argues. 'The first duty of any pastor is to have an accurate, fair and documented picture of the heresies in his patch – and a *wise* pastor may often prefer not to shout about them from the roof-top.'

Kerr accepts that it is easy to identify all manner of superstition in some non-Christian belief systems; but dismisses Ratzinger's negative reference to anonymous Christianity as 'little more than a smear'. If properly explained, the phrase (which derives from Rahner) 'illuminate[s] perfectly genuine ecclesiological issues'. The same might be said, *mutatis mutandis*, for the Cardinal's dim view of feminist theology. Admittedly, some who march under this banner are their own worst enemies. Others, though, are refreshing the tradition in vital respects. As Kerr puts it: 'it is surprising how the few efforts that there have so far been to retrieve the feminine and maternal images of God . . . in the Bible and in the tradition have revealed a quite widespread, unwittingly idolatrous attachment to the masculine [gender], among women as well as among men.'

The historian Eamon Duffy begins his contribution[10] to the *New Blackfriars* symposium by accepting that authentic discipleship must be counter-cultural. In many areas of life – economic relations, defence and foreign aid policies, and sexual and family morality – a gospel-based stance would be unlikely to endear Christians to society at large. 'Bourgeois individualism and materialism *do* have an unhappy hold over Catholics, both individually and corporately, and there is certainly much in the culture of post-conciliar Catholicism that owes more to . . . California than to Jerusalem or Rome.'

But he identifies hermeneutical naivety in Ratzinger's distinction between the deposit of faith and culturally conditioned perspectives imposed on it in Latin America, the United States, Africa and other parts of the world. 'Who, where,' Duffy asks, 'has ever had access to an eternal gospel *not* subject in some fundamental sense to the particularities of time and place and circumstance?' Behind this criticism lies an insight that Newman, among others, was at pains to point out: that the relation of the Church to truth is not miraculous – 'breaking through the limitations of earthly existence', as Duffy puts it – but sacramental – that is, speaking to us precisely in and through those limitations.

In his essay, 'Catholic theology and the crisis of classicism',[11]

Nicholas Lash puts the debate in a larger theoretical framework with reference to what he describes as one of Newman's most neglected major works, the 1877 Preface to *The Via Media of the Anglican Church*. This pictures Christianity as 'at once a philosophy, a political power and a religious rite', and each of these three constitutive aspects as having a particular institutional focus: learning and reflection in the schools of theology; order and organisation in the papacy and other mechanisms of government; and experience and devotion in the local community of 'pastor and flock'. Central to Newman's account is his refusal to allocate to any one of these three 'offices' a position of privilege or centrality in respect of the others. As Lash explains:

> the health of the Church consists in the permanently precarious *equilibrium* of all three of its constitutive aspects or principles. This equilibrium is lost when any one of the three 'offices' achieves a position of dominance . . . What Newman's sketch especially helps us to see . . . is that it is to be *expected* that this relationship will be one of tension and, frequently, of friction.

So the lesson not absorbed in Ratzinger's 'classicist' analysis is that a Church without restlessness would be a mausoleum. Lash goes on to question another of the Cardinal's bluntly expressed claims, that 'the best values that two hundred years of "liberal" culture had produced' have now, 'suitably purified and corrected', been appropriated by the Church. 'I wish I shared his confidence,' Lash continues. 'High amongst such values, surely, is the conviction that, when power is opposed to rationality, or when disputes are settled by power at the expense of justice, then both truth and human dignity suffer. And yet, one of the standing scandals of twentieth-century Catholicism has been the "one-sidedness" of the relationship between theology and governance.'

John Mahoney's contribution is simply entitled 'On the other hand . . .'.[12] He regrets Ratzinger's conflation of the moral experience of the Church with its magisterium 'in ways which [Vatican II] would not have recognised'. Could it not be that the role of moral theology within the Church 'is more positively an intermediary one between the Gospel values and modern culture?' Noting the Cardinal's concern that bishops' conferences, as well as moral theologians, are drawing too close to mainstream society, Mahoney cites Ratzinger's very different view of the matter in his

1965 *Concilium* article already quoted. Mahoney's essay wrestles with some highly complex questions in canon law before a coda blending theological and pastoral elements. It concludes, among other things, that a mentality of diocesan centralisation, almost as much as Roman centralisation, can impede true collegial action; and that no diocese today is an island. 'The "good of the Church" identifiable at regional or national level calls for an identifying and exercise of collegial jurisdiction at that level . . . Here is the ultimate "theological foundation" for episcopal conferences, which Cardinal Ratzinger is at pains now to deny.'

* * *

So much, then, for the Prefect's antagonistic streak. *Salt of the Earth* and *God and the World* are milder. An Augustinian outlook is still in evidence – Ratzinger even declines to endorse John Paul II's view of the third millennium as a springtime of the human spirit[13] – but the Cardinal also sounds humbler. At one point, for instance, Seewald asks him whether he might not in retrospect have treated figures such as Küng and Boff too harshly, even supposing the criticisms of their work was right, and Ratzinger immediately acknowledges fault on his part. 'I would distinguish between my personal reactions and what we did officially. That in a personal controversy I occasionally react too harshly, I concede [straightaway]. But in what we did as a congregation, I think that we kept to the right measure.'[14] He restates his view that liberation theology during the 1970s and 80s entailed 'a politicisation of the faith that would have forced it into an irresponsible political partisanship', and claims that Gutiérrez, in particular, benefited from 'dialogue' with the CDF by seeing the 'one-sidedness' of his work and then developing it 'further in the direction of a suitable form of liberation theology that really had a future'.[15]

Seewald points out that 'dialogue' included the imposition of a 'penitential silence' in Boff's case. Ratzinger's reply again reveals a perhaps unexpected capacity for self-criticism. He says that this measure might be inappropriate or redundant, but adds that 'objectively considered, it wasn't bad to invite someone to reflect longer on a difficult question. Perhaps it would do us all some good were someone to tell us, "you should stop talking about that for a while, you shouldn't keep publishing frenetically, but give things a chance to mature." '[16]

The line of questioning is sustained in a manner that is objective but not disrespectful. Asked whether an analogy he once drew between sex and a 'floating mine' doesn't reflect an unhealthy view of physical love, Ratzinger gives a revealing reply (even though he is badly served by his translator):

> I meant that it is indeed the great forces that, when torn away from their human center, can also be the most destructive. Sexuality forms man's entire bodiliness, whether male or female. Precisely because it is great and because man can't become mature without it, can't even become himself, it moulds the person most deeply. However, when sexuality escapes man's unity, it can also tear him apart and destroy him.

At least part of *The Ratzinger Report*, including its verdict on the Marxist cul-de-sac, has been vindicated by events. Seewald accepts this, but reminds Ratzinger that the point is not as widely granted as he might expect. 'Is this,' he asks, 'due to the certainty with which you defend your standpoint, to the severity of your language?' The Cardinal replies that:

> when things turn out in a certain way, a lot of people do not remember that they actually confirm diagnoses that I had made. I tend to believe that it is due to the identification of my person with the office of the Prefect and to the concomitant aversion toward its whole function and toward the Magisterium as such. So a lot of people read everything I may say as part of a mechanism . . . to keep mankind in tutelage and not as a genuine, honest, intellectual attempt to understand the world and man.[17]

This and other arguments point back towards first principles, and Seewald also asks about the coherence of Christianity in *God and the World*. He records an attitude common among enquirers – that Christianity offers a questionable answer to a real problem – and he reveals that 'although I had doubts and mistrusted messages of salvation, it still seemed to me beyond contradiction that the world was no accident nor the result of an explosion or something like that, as Marx and others maintained. And certainly not the creation of man, who can neither cure the common cold, nor stop a dam from breaking.'[18] Talking to Ratzinger (now hailed

in the book's preface as 'one of the Church's great wise men'), he
began to see a correlation between 'the web of worship, prayer,
and commandments' and the 'mysterious truth' that he appre-
hended, but could not name. Seewald adds that the process of his
return to the Christian fold was incremental, but it could be
summed up in a lapidary remark of the Cardinal: 'Creation bears
within itself an order. We can work out from this the ideas of God
– and even the right way for us to live.'[19]

At the outset, Seewald raises chestnuts such as Catholicism and
guilt. Ratzinger replies that baroque and rococo art are marked
by a great sense of joy, that Catholic societies such as Italy and
Spain are rightly famed for light-heartedness, and that undue
rigour is foreign to the true spirit of the faith. Catholics should be
animated, above all, 'by a great sense of God's forgiveness'. Then
he is asked how God communicates with him. The Cardinal replies
that God speaks quietly.

> But he gives us all kinds of signs. In retrospect, especially, we
> can see that he has given us a little nudge through a friend,
> through a book, or through what we see as a failure – even
> through 'accidents'. Life is actually full of these silent indica-
> tions. If I remain alert, then slowly they piece together a
> consistent whole, and I begin to feel how God is guiding me.[20]

Ratzinger then underlines the importance of fun as a fount of
spiritual growth, and says that God has a great sense of humour.
'Sometimes he gives you something like a nudge and says, Don't
take yourself so seriously . . . God wants to prod us into taking
things a bit more lightly; to see the funny side; to get down off our
pedestal . . .'[21]

The man who has so often been likened to a Grand Inquisitor
also acknowledges a place for frustration, and even anger, during
periods of spiritual aridity: 'The voice of Job remains an authentic
voice, which also tells us that we may do the same.' A Christian
acting like Job will therefore see a problem as an opportunity,
Ratzinger avers: 'Seneca the stoic said: Sympathy is abhorrent. If,
on the other hand, we look at Christ, he is all sympathy, and that
makes him precious to us. Being sympathetic, being vulnerable, is
part of being a Christian. One must learn to accept injuries, to
live with wounds, and in the end to find therein a deeper
healing.'[22]

The conversation then deals at more length with the metaphysical implications of these insights. Seewald quotes a remark of Ratzinger on an earlier occasion: 'If a person believes only what he can see with his own eyes, then really he is blind.' 'Because in that case,' the Cardinal now explains, 'he is limiting his horizon in such a fashion that the essential things escape him. He cannot after all see his own understanding. Precisely those things that are of real moment are what he does not see with the mere physical eye, and to that extent he cannot properly see if he cannot see beyond his immediate sensory perceptions.'[23]

The move towards full Christian commitment may be (and was in his own case) more like silent growth than a leap, Ratzinger recalls. It involves swimming in and out of the shallow water at first, and gradually getting a sense 'of the ocean that is coming in toward us'. Then he expresses the insight that faith is not a possession: 'I also think that one has never achieved complete faith. Faith has to be lived again and again in life and in suffering, as well as in the great joys that God sends us. It is never something that I can put in my pocket like a coin.'[24]

God and the World covers the gamut of Christian belief, including the doctrine of the incarnation. Ratzinger begins by pointing out that this fundamental Christian teaching tends to be viewed with particular scepticism in Asia, where God is thought of as being 'so immeasurable', and our capacity to conceive him 'so limited'. Then he exposes a logical flaw in this argument. It places an unwitting constraint on the Almighty, because 'humility would turn to pride if we were to deny God the freedom and the power and the love' to make himself as small as a man: 'The Christian faith brings us exactly [this] consolation, that God is so great that he can become small . . . It is just in this that we actually see the truly infinite nature of God, for this is more powerful, more inconceivable than anything else, and at the same time more saving.' Such a doctrine, he infers, 'is exactly what we need' to avoid having to live with 'fragments and half-truths'.[25]

Later the Cardinal expounds Catholic eucharistic doctrine, another difficult and frequently misinterpreted area. Transubstantiation is the process by which the Lord irrevocably takes possession of the consecrated bread and wine. This does not entail a claim about physics: 'It has never been asserted that . . . nature in a physical sense is being changed. The transformation reaches down to a more profound level. Tradition has it that this is a metaphysical process.'[26]

Two other noteworthy components of *God and the World* are Ratzinger's defence of contentious articles of church teaching, and his eirenic attitude towards non-Christians. For example, he advances a serious argument against the use of condoms. Where people accept the importance of marriage and fidelity, 'then children have a sphere of life in which they can learn love and self-restraint . . . The misery comes, not from the large families, but from the irresponsible and undisciplined procreation of children who have no father, and often no mother . . .' Yet the force of this argument is blunted by hyperbole, as he then describes the use of contraception as a 'mechanistic' substitute for morality: 'Misery comes from demoralizing society, not from moralizing it, and the condom propaganda is an essential part of this demoralizing, the expression of an attitude that despises people and that in any case thinks people capable of nothing good whatsoever.'[27] Some of his other arguments show a similar lack of finesse. He appears to beg the question when he says that 'the basic structural pattern of human existence is being violated' when gay partnerships are granted 'equal status' with marriage. But his abiding concern is to defend the 'public and social' character of marriage as the best framework for child-rearing.

Ratzinger's generous side emerges when he is asked to gloss canon 849 of the Code of Canon Law, which states that 'Baptism . . . [is] necessary to salvation in fact or at least in intention.' Asked what happens to people who die unbaptised (a large majority of humanity), or to aborted foetuses, the Cardinal quotes the Vatican declaration that those 'who are seeking for God and who are inwardly striving toward that which constitutes baptism will also receive salvation'. Tradition has often held that unbaptised babies (born or unborn) will enjoy the state of natural blessedness known as limbo, but Ratzinger applauds John Paul II for stretching this belief by suggesting in his 1995 encyclical *Evangelium Vitae* that 'God is powerful enough to draw to himself all those who were unable to receive the sacrament.'[28]

During the final sections of the book, in a series of answers that caused surprise in some quarters, Ratzinger also holds out a friendly hand to the lapsed and to half-believers, arguing that the Church cannot be for spiritual athletes alone.

It was to a very small community at the time, the disciples, that Jesus said that they had to be the yeast and the salt of the earth. That assumes they are small. But it also assumes that they have a responsibility to the whole . . . I have nothing against . . . people who all year long never visit a church [but] go there at least on Christmas Night or New Year's Eve or on special occasions, because this is another way of belonging to the blessing of the sacred, to the light. There have to be various forms of participation and association; the Church has to be inwardly open.[29]

God and the World ends on a soaring note, demonstrating the Prefect's capacity to assume the role of a prophet. Asked whether he would agree with John XXIII's comment that he belonged to 'a Church that is alive and young and that is carrying her work on fearlessly into the future', Ratzinger gives a positive reply. 'I can indeed see many old and dying branches in the Church, which are slowly dropping off . . .' But above all else he can see the 'youth of the Church'. He is 'able to meet so many young people' from around the world; and so many adherents of the new lay movements, whose 'enthusiasm of faith' is making its mark. 'And this enthusiasm cannot be shaken by any of the criticisms of the Church – which always have some basis – because . . . the Lord will quite obviously not abandon her.'[30]

7

The Turn of the Screw

That *The Ratzinger Report* amounted to far more than *propos de vacances* is borne out by the case studies discussed in Chapter 5. And although the prophetic edge demonstrated by *Salt of the Earth* and *God and the World* is perhaps an accurate sign of how a Ratzinger papacy might unfold, it was as an enforcer that he chiefly operated until Pope John Paul's death. The strike against dissent became progressively more evident from around 1990, and applied to theologians as a class, not only to individuals.

There was relatively little concerted opposition, despite occasional attempts to reverse the restorationist tide, such as the Cologne Declaration, issued in January 1989. Signed by more than one hundred and fifty German-speaking theologians, including Norbert Greinacher (a Tübingen professor), Häring, Metz and Küng, and later by hundreds more from elsewhere in Europe, the declaration accuses John Paul of exceeding his powers by muzzling scholars and appointing bishops 'without respecting the suggestions of the local churches'. In particular, the signatories deplore the withholding of official licences from some university teachers, which they interpret as 'a dangerous intrusion into the freedom of research and training'. The declaration goes on to say that John Paul and his aides have been wrong to insist on the unchallengeable position of Vatican statements.

The counter-attack was uncompromising. Less than two months later, new declarations of loyalty were introduced for holders of certain offices. The Profession of Faith consists of the Nicene Creed (an existing requirement) plus a declaration of adherence to wider church teaching; and the Oath of Fidelity is an expanded version of an undertaking previously given only by bishops. In May 1990, as we have seen, the CDF produced its most detailed assertion of theology's auxiliary status vis-à-vis officialdom in its 'Instruction on the Ecclesial Vocation of the Theologian'. This represents a compressed statement of the vision Ratzinger was to spell out in his book *The Nature and Mission of Theology*.[1] He concedes that Catholic scholarship and the magisterium perform discrete functions, but maintains that the magisterium traces boundaries that scholarship must not breach. Only by accepting 'authentic' parameters can theology be true to its own frames of reference. In a statement at this time, the Cardinal effectively said that the Instruction was necessary because theologians had got above themselves. Scholars in the post-conciliar period had arrogated to themselves the role of 'true teachers of the Church and even of the bishops', and often trumpeted their views through the press.

The document begins by denying that the collective mind of the faithful – the *sensus fidelium* – can serve as a counterweight to the hierarchy. Citing *Lumen Gentium*, it interprets the *sensus fidelium* more in terms of stewardship, defining the term as 'universal' consent on matters of faith and morals shared by a company 'from the bishops to the last of the faithful'. In an echo of G. K. Chesterton's maxim that tradition is the democracy of the dead, the Instruction describes Catholic faith as 'diachronic', meaning it extends across time as well as space. Academic freedom and magisterial authority are not opposed forces, because authentic research, 'which the academic community rightly holds most precious', involves accepting 'the methodology corresponding to the object under study'. Theology's object is divine revelation, 'handed on and interpreted in the Church under the authority of the magisterium, and received by faith. These givens have the force of principles. To eliminate them would mean to cease doing theology.'

Elsewhere, the Instruction exhorts bishops to exercise greater watchfulness against contaminations of the faith, and reasserts that 'definitive' teaching must be accepted, even if it has not been promulgated *ex cathedra*. In common with similar publications, though, the document has a circular quality (it assumes that the point at issue is already universally accepted). Critics again questioned the appropriateness of unstinting loyalty, given the Church's past mistakes. Ratzinger, addressing this matter at a press conference, said that some of the magisterium's decisions could not be the final word on a given topic, but might be classed as 'provisional policy' based on 'permanent . . . principles'. The Instruction itself shows some awareness of the dilemma faced by a theologian who believes that Vatican teaching is wrong. 'For a loyal spirit, animated by love for the Church, such a situation can certainly prove a difficult trial. It can be a call to suffer for the truth, in silence and prayer, but with a certainty that if the truth really is at stake, it will ultimately prevail.' Meanwhile, private judgement is not to be sanctified by conscience: 'setting up a supreme magisterium of conscience in opposition to the magisterium of the Church means adopting a principle of free examination incompatible with the economy of revelation . . .'

This is not the moment for a systematic critique of Ratzinger's thinking, but the outline of a challenge might run as follows. As an Augustinian, he believes that human beings are bearers of an inner light, even though it is shadowed by sin. This light (in Hegel's words) is 'the candle of the Lord': it originates outside us and is a mark of our created dignity. When an Anglican thinker such as Hooker defended the integrity of balancing Scripture, tradition and reason, it was with this model of the human constitution in mind. Even though his target was sixteenth-century Puritan hubris, the assumptions Hooker criticised live on in the Catholic as well as the Reformation traditions. They are based on confusion of the visible and invisible Church, and of the beliefs and aspirations Christians legitimately share with ways in which they try to embody them.

Arguments of this kind fell on deaf ears in Rome. Ratzinger's campaign to buttress the vision he shared with John Paul was unflagging for the remainder of his period as Prefect. As we have seen, *Ad Tuendam Fidem* and *Dominus Iesus* are, among other things, zealous statements of *romanità*, or a centralising ideology. So is *Apostolos Suos* (the 1998 declaration that bars episcopal conferences from publishing statements on faith or morals which are not either agreed unanimously or issued with Rome's advance approval). In *Witness to Hope*, his official biography of John Paul, George Weigel writes that *Apostolos Suos* was widely misjudged in the media. It was simply a tightening-up exercise, predicated on 'a basic theological truth taught by Vatican II', that the college of bishops exercises authority under its head, the Pope. If the Church is a communion, Weigel goes on, 'then the question of the relationship of national conferences of bishops to the Bishop of

Rome cannot be understood as one in which the conferences' "gain" is the papacy's "loss." '[2]

Others were unpersuaded. In an article entitled 'Power to the Bishops',[3] Ladislas Orsy, a canon lawyer based at Georgetown University in Washington, DC, portrayed his theme as pivotal to the meaning and legacy of Vatican II. He identifies two mutually exclusive interpretations of the relevant sections of *Lumen Gentium*. According to the centralising or 'Roman' view, 'partial gatherings of the bishops, legitimate as they may be, such as particular councils, synods, and conferences, have no collegial power.' The second perspective noted by Orsy holds that 'whenever a group of bishops gather – in communion with their brother bishops and the bishop of Rome – to fulfil their pastoral task, they also act as a college, and have a collective power in the proper sense of the term, although not in its fullness.' This, he explains, arises from the doctrine of participation: 'we hold that the pope has the authentic power of primacy even when he teaches with lesser authority or gives directives less formally. We do not contend, ever, that he is speaking and acting in the mere "spirit of primacy", or that he is exercising only "affective primacy". Rather, he always has authority but does not always use it fully.'

Orsy points out that the departments of the Holy See never cease to stress that 'they somehow participate in the power of the primacy although not fully.' Yet they 'deny that the episcopal conferences could have true collegial power but not fully'. Moreover, if the Vatican II Fathers had intended to affirm no more than the Roman view, it is impossible to understand why the subject was debated so heatedly at the time, and the result described as a misfortune (*'sfortuna'*) by Cardinal Ottaviani. If, though (Orsy continues), we accept that the Council intended something more, then 'logically it follows that the first theory is not an interpretation but a "nullification" of [Vatican II's] doctrine of episcopal collegiality.' Orsy also sees a trinitarian dimension to debate on church government. Since Christians believe the fount of all reality to be a communion of divine persons, then the Church might better reflect its source through a more representative style of leadership.

Before looking further at the pastoral implications of such debate, it is worth perservering with principles for a moment longer. The connection between trinitarian doctrine and arguments about democracy in the Church is not always immediately obvious outside clerical circles, but Orsy's final remark is of the utmost importance. In essence, he means that Ratzinger's advocacy of Roman centralism is a tell-tale mark of a defective model of God, under which diversity is trumped by unity. Protestant critics of Ratzinger's views, including the Yale-based Croatian theologian Miroslav Volf,[4] have tended to agree.

This is the context in which the Cardinal was rebuked by Walter Kasper on the eve of the new millennium. The then Bishop of Rottenburg-Stuttgart attacked a CDF document, 'The Church as Communion', published several years earlier. This text, according to Kasper, amounted to 'more or less a reversal' of Vatican II. He supported his case through a closer look at the terms 'Church' and 'Universal Church'. Kasper holds that in the Acts of the Apostles, Luke presents the original Christian community in Jerusalem as both universal and local: 'that is his perspective, though historically there were presumably several communities from the beginning: besides the one in Jerusalem, there were several in Galilee. The one Church therefore consisted of local Churches from the beginning.' But for the CDF text, according to Kasper, the universal Church ('stealthily identified with the Roman Church, and de facto with the Pope and Curia') somehow precedes its manifestations at a local level.[5]

Ratzinger replied somewhat tetchily to this in the *Frankfurter Allgemeine Zeitung* on 22 December 2000. 'For theologians who think anything of themselves today it seems to have become a duty to criticise CDF documents negatively,' he wrote. Turning to the subject under dispute, he went on: 'it is precisely when one identifies the local church in Jerusalem at the beginning with the universal Church that this temptation arises. For then the definition of the Church has already been reduced to the communities which make it up empirically and its theological depth has been lost.'

For Kasper (who answered Ratzinger in the Munich-based monthly *Stimmen der Zeit*), this argument seems to assume that the 'Universal' Church exists in a quasi-Platonic space apart from its manifestation in history. But the conflict extends beyond the question of Rome's relation to the rest of the Catholic world. As a keen ecumenist, Kasper emphasises that 'the ultimate ecumenical aim is not a uniform united Church, but one Church in reconciled diversity . . . We can only represent this aim credibly if in our own Church we are exemplary in showing that the universal

Church and the local Church are related as unity in diversity and diversity in unity.'[6] By this time, and to the surprise of many, Kasper had been promoted to the post of Secretary (or deputy) at the Vatican's ecumenical office, the Pontifical Council for Promoting Christian Unity, shortly before its President, Cardinal Edward Cassidy, was to retire. Kasper succeeded him, and received a red hat of his own in early 2001.

* * *

The Ratzinger–Kasper dispute also boils down to a question about the validity and extent of local discretion in decisions over second-order issues of belief and practice. There were several assorted causes célèbres in this area during the 1990s and since, including the historic accord between Lutherans and Catholics on justification, the so-called church crisis in Austria, and a battle between Rome and several episcopal conferences over the authorisation of liturgical change. Ratzinger was involved in all of them to some degree.

During his Stuttgart years, Kasper and two other senior figures, Bishop Karl Lehmann of Mainz and Archbishop Oskar Saier of Freiburg, had petitioned the Vatican in 1994 on behalf of remarried divorcees, arguing that the rule forbidding them from taking communion should be relaxed under certain circumstances. The refusal of their request was a source of lasting anguish to all three. An analogous situation arose several years later when John Paul and Ratzinger sought to end official Catholic involvement in a counselling service for women in Germany contemplating abortions. A countrywide law allows terminations within the first three months of pregnancy, provided that a woman has received counselling at one of 1700 licensed advice centres, about 270 of which were run by the Catholic Church before the turn of the millennium. The rationale for official Christian involvement was simple. By persuading as many women as possible not to end their pregnancies, Catholic advisers were helping to save the lives of many unborn children – 5000 a year on average. But opponents warned that since a woman intent on a termination could still receive the green light from a church-run centre, its staff would be colluding in grave sin.

In January 1998, John Paul wrote to the German bishops with a tough (some said impossible) demand: that they continue to provide resources for advising needy women, while ceasing to issue the certificates with which abortions could be procured. One compromise floated was that the legal status of the certificates should be downgraded through an extra clause saying that they could not be used to end pregnancies. Supporters of the status quo felt that this would be severely counter-productive. It would deter many women from going to church-run establishments in the first place, and generate a clutch of fresh legal problems. The authorities in Germany's various *Länder* were likely to take different views of the clause, depending on levels of deference to the Church. More generally, the counselling system had been introduced nationwide only in response to church lobbying. The former East Germany had sanctioned abortion on demand. There were also ecumenical implications: Catholics and Protestants had hitherto provided a united witness through the existing system.

Senior clerics were deeply split. The more liberal bishops expressed strong reluctance to change course. Karl Lehmann, also president of the country's episcopal conference, urged Ratzinger and the Pope to reconsider, while conservatives in the German hierarchy supported the CDF view. The disagreement extended to the highest reaches of the Vatican. The Secretary of State, Cardinal Sodano, for example, agreed that Church–state relations in Germany might suffer substantial damage through a change in policy. The centres were closed in 2000, but John Paul and Ratzinger's victory was qualified. Grassroots opposition to Rome's stance greatly exceeded that of the bishops. Outraged by what they saw as an assault on Christian witness, lay Catholics formed a body called Donum Vitae (The Gift of Life) to continue providing the same service as hitherto. Donum Vitae establishments have functioned well in some parts of the country, including Bavaria and North Rhine-Westphalia, but enjoyed far less success elsewhere.

This episode provides a notable example of Ratzinger's long-felt ambivalence towards the Catholic Church in Germany, and throws a sidelight on his part in the appointment of unpopular hardliners to vacant sees there. His sometimes tense relations with his fellow countrymen also resulted in a rare public humiliation for him at this time. It happened at the 2001 Consistory, before which two batches of new cardinals were announced, the second appearing like an afterthought, and including Lehmann.

The first group (Kasper among them) were named in mid-January. Commentators had hardly had time to express their disappointment that Lehmann had once again been passed over when he received a phone call with news of his elevation. The cardinal-to-be assumed that the papal nuncio was joking.

A number of theories have been floated to explain what seems like evidence of muddle, and even panic, in the Vatican. For Robert Leicht, a former Editor of the German weekly *Die Zeit*, the episode demonstrated that 'even the Pope is not absolutely sovereign and totally independent of the need to elicit a consensus'.[7] There is some truth in this, but the signs of a stifled struggle suggest another explanation. Sources in Germany and the Vatican have told me that Ratzinger fought 'very hard' to prevent Lehmann's appointment, but this time he met his match in Archbishop Alfons Nossol of Opole in Poland, a close adviser of John Paul and a personal friend of Lehmann. (Nossol is half German, and had earlier declined an invitation to take up a senior Vatican post on the grounds that his energies were better deployed in a pastoral job.) The inclusion of a relative free-thinker among the new cardinals followed a long phone conversation between the Pope and his confidant. At the Consistory Mass several weeks later, it was widely noted that Sodano embraced Lehmann warmly during the kiss of peace, while Ratzinger's greeting was monosyllabic.

* * *

Attempts to extend lay participation in the Austrian Church during the 1990s were especially ill-fated, and their outcomes are often cited among the symptoms of an underlying malaise. The initiative emerged from a sex scandal. In 1995, the Archbishop of Vienna, Cardinal Hans Hermann Groer, was publicly accused of sexually assaulting novices in his care during the 1960s and 70s, and even of having asked some of them to undress in the confessional. As a Benedictine, he had lived an enclosed life before his surprise appointment as Austria's Primate in 1986. The crisis was worsened by two factors. Groer's predecessor, Cardinal Franz König, had a maximalist understanding of Vatican II, and was widely admired as a generous pastor. 'König changed the Church,' comments Christa Pongratz-Lippitt, Vienna correspondent of *The Tablet*, who knew the Cardinal well during his later years.

He helped large numbers of Austrian Catholics wake up to the fact that they had long been treated like sheep. He went out into the world and said, 'Even agnostics and atheists have a lot to contribute. They're estranged from us and we need to listen to their experience.' He didn't condemn. This marked a great break with the past.

For his pains, König incurred Rome's displeasure during the early 1980s, especially through his acceptance of conscience as a commanding factor in sexual morality. The Vatican seemed intent on teaching the Austrian Church a lesson by parachuting hardliners into top posts, and Groer's preferment – along with that of the grossly ill-mannered and tactless Kurt Krenn, who became Bishop of Sankt Pölten in 1991 – formed part of a pattern. Both men were much disliked, and assumed to have got their jobs by dint of ardent loyalty to Rome. Second, however, Groer at first remained silent in the face of the accusations, and only issued a highly equivocal apology in 1998. Even his successor, Cardinal Christoph Schönborn, said that he was almost certainly guilty.

A statute of limitation saved the accused (who died in 2003) from arrest and trial. But what chiefly shocked observers was that the Church took no steps to launch an investigation of its own. Lay groups, clustering under the banner of We are Church, the international umbrella group for reformers, were sufficiently nettled to stage a referendum in 1995 in which 500,000 people voted for measures such as voluntary clerical celibacy, the admission of women to church offices, a greater local say in episcopal nominations, and a reform of teaching on sexual ethics. These goals were restated – and endorsed with large majorities – during the 'Dialogue for Austria', an initiative launched during a major conference at Salzburg in 1998.

The Austrian Church's 'long Good Friday', as König called it, is a labyrinthine business well chronicled in sections of the press. It has involved pig-headedness in the Vatican (which also refused to comment on the Groer case: John Paul did not even mention it, still less offer an apology, during his visit to Austria in 1998) and a widespread perception of poor judgement on the part of successive papal nuncios in Vienna, especially Archbishops Michele Cecchini and Donato Squicciarini. Many observers also point a finger at Cardinal Alfons Stickler, an intensely conservative Austrian and former Vatican Librarian, who still resides in Rome, and has influenced the appointments process to some degree. The sense that parts of the hierarchy were in collective denial over the crisis was corroborated when the Archbishop of Cologne, Cardinal Joachim Meisner (another personal friend of Ratzinger), was dispatched to conduct Groer's funeral. Meisner's homily gave the impression that his fellow cardinal was a martyr.

Ratzinger's direct and tangential roles in the affair relate to his membership of the Congregation for Bishops, and his implacable hostility to the We are Church movement, signalled in two leaked letters he wrote to the president of the Austrian episcopal conference, Bishop Johann Weber of Graz-Seckau, in 1997.[8] After meeting in early 1999, the Austrian bishops announced that their discussions had focused on the Dialogue and its aims. But then the CDF published a document, signed by Ratzinger, describing the reformist platform as an unacceptable deviation. The Congregation and two other Vatican departments also took steps to discipline Bishop Paul Iby of Eisenstadt, who met pro-Dialogue campaigners in his diocese, and drew up resolutions based on the encounter. According to Paul Zulehner, Professor of Pastoral Theology at Vienna University, Iby was obliged to 'correct' them 'without mentioning that he had been instructed to do so by Rome'.[9]

König died in early 2004, and Ratzinger came to preside at his requiem. The grand old man of the Austrian Church hadn't been asked to concelebrate with the other bishops during the 1998 papal visit to his country six years earlier; so the Prefect's presence was interpreted as a fence-mending gesture. During his homily, Ratzinger made what struck many as an overdue admission: that the CDF might sometimes have acted too severely. 'I thought, "My dear man, you're too late to make it up to König: he's gone to heaven," ' Christa Pongratz-Lippitt recalls. 'Ratzinger appeared old and sick – almost a broken figure – during the service, but gave a stronger performance at the press conference afterwards. This was when he rehearsed his familiar message about the changing times. Bishops had needed to embrace the world in the 1960s, but a new kind of leadership was required thereafter.'

Many lesser instances of animosity between Rome and local Churches could be cited. Even the Archbishop of Westminster, Cardinal Basil Hume, felt persecuted for his relatively relaxed style of leadership in England and Wales, and clashed with Archbishop Bertone in 1998 when the CDF sought to censure Sr

Lavinia Byrne, a London-based teacher and broadcaster. Hume held off the hawks while he was still alive, but his death in mid-1999 cleared the way for tougher action against her. Byrne, who had written in support of women's ordination, later left her order.

In Germany, Bishop Franz Xaver Eder of Passau published a pastoral plan for his diocese, 'Close to God and to Human Beings' (*Gott und den Menschen Nahe*), in 2000. Even though he had decreed in advance that its terms of reference should not extend beyond local issues, the plan was based on extensive consultations among lay Catholics. The diocesan offices received 50,000 requests for copies. On reaching his seventy-fifth birthday soon afterwards, Bishop Eder automatically submitted his resignation to Rome. It was accepted at once (bishops in good odour with the Vatican are usually required to remain in post for longer if their health permits it). Though not asked to clamp down on reformers, he was warned in a confidential letter from Rome of the 'danger' posed by 'liberal and humanistically degenerate churchgoers'.[10]

Eder's successor was Bishop Wilhelm Schraml, auxiliary in the Regensburg diocese and a friend of Ratzinger. German observers across the board have described Schraml to me as a narrow-minded and anxious figure. During his first year in Passau, he closed the office responsible for pastoral outreach, and informed the diocesan council that it would be sent a topped and tailed pastoral plan not based on consultation. Zulehner also sees this episode in a negative light, and argues that 'as part of his curtailment programme', Schraml 'redefined the term "pastoral plan", [promising] to continue it. What he meant was that he would continue with it, but in the manner of a clerically led and not participatory church.'[11]

The United States saw persistent debate on authority during this period. A snapshot of the situation came during the 1999 annual convention of the Catholic Theological Society of America, held in Miami, at which Fr (later Cardinal) Avery Dulles SJ accused an increasing number of dissenters of refusing to grant popes and councils a role in defining revealed truths. He suggested that for such theologians, revelation is 'an ecstatic encounter with God that has no doctrinal content'. Accepting that it was legitimate to debate the limits of infallibility, he never-theless denounced 'aggressive patterns' of division and 'a general climate in which dissent from non-infallible doctrine is considered courageous, authentic, and forward-looking, while submission is

viewed as cowardly, hypocritical, and retrograde'. He also condemned 'those who go to the extremes of organized resistance'
by 'recruiting a constituency, calling press conferences...
soliciting signatures to petitions, and setting themselves up as a
kind of alternative' to the Church's teaching authority.[12] But for
Dulles's fellow Jesuit Fr Richard McCormick, the fault lay with
Vatican officials, who acted as if all doctrines except social
teachings were set in stone. If public dissent had become a
problem, he said, this was largely because John Paul had denied
the possibility of authentic development.

* * *

Ecumenically, Ratzinger's office displayed a certain skittishness,
as well as apparent authoritarianism. On 25 June 1998, for
example, an elated Cardinal Cassidy presented the Joint Declaration on the Doctrine of Justification by the Holy See and the
World Lutheran Federation. This text lists dozens of areas in
which either full accord or high degress of consensus have been
reached, and includes the historic avowal that 'By grace alone, in
faith in Christ's saving work and not because of any merit on our
part, we are accepted by God and receive the Holy Spirit, who
renews our hearts while equipping... and calling us to good
works.' In a statement to journalists, Cassidy said: 'It must be
considered without doubt an outstanding achievement of the
ecumenical movement and a milestone on the way to restoration
of full, visible unity among the disciples of... Christ.'

Yet it soon appeared as though he was being undermined by
his own side. The CDF published a response to the accord almost
at once, arguing that the Lutheran doctrine of justification is
incompatible with Roman Catholic teaching on the consequences
of baptism. The response (almost certainly written by Ratzinger,
or produced with his involvement) went on to question whether
the World Lutheran Federation really had the authority to speak
for all its members.

This led to supefaction on both sides, and almost derailed the
accord's formal ratification. But Cassidy fought his corner
tenaciously behind the scenes. In June 1999, he relaunched the
accord together with an 'annex' answering the CDF response
point by point. Writing soon afterwards to the *Frankfurter
Allgemeine Zeitung*, Ratzinger strongly denied that he had torpe-

doed the accord, and in November of that year he took part in a deal-saving summit held at his brother's house in Regensburg. The Lutheran side was represented by Bishop Johannes Hanselmann and Professor Joachim Track. Ratzinger evidently made some important concessions, among them an acceptance that the broader purpose of ecumenism is unity in diversity, not necessarily 'structural reintegration'. Bishop George Anderson, the senior Lutheran leader in the United States, told the *National Catholic Reporter* that 'it was Ratzinger who untied the knots . . . Without him we might not have an agreement.'[13]

Anglicans never faced a roller-coaster of this kind, but also detected a fickle side to CDF procedures. Established in 1970, the first Anglican–Roman Catholic International Commission (ARCIC I) produced its *Final Report*, dealing with eucharistic doctrine, ministry and authority, in 1982. This received a cool – and in places incoherent – response soon after Ratzinger's appointment as Prefect, as did several later joint statements on other subjects. 'I found Cardinal Ratzinger very intelligent and courteous,' comments Bishop Mark Santer, Anglican co-chairman of ARCIC from 1983 to 1999, 'and always very willing to concede a point, as well as to make one. Some of his comments were very pertinent.'

Yet when Santer and his colleagues were in Rome during the mid-1980s to discuss another ecumenical text, *Salvation and the Church*, they found that Ratzinger's advisers had not understood ARCIC's methods. 'Our aim had been to go behind polemical Reformation language in search of a common understanding,' Santer explains. 'We found that the CDF was demanding univocal declarations that weren't possible in our view. I was reminded of conservative Evangelicals who insist that everything one says today has to be squared with the wording of the Thirty-Nine Articles. If you have this cast of mind, you run the risk of letting big opportunities slip away.'

ARCIC II nevertheless produced a further statement, *The Gift of Authority*, in 1999, which suggested that the Anglicans might be prepared to accord a universal primacy to bishops of Rome. And with Benedict's election, the Archbishop of Canterbury, among others, is far from gloomy about the future. 'There's every chance now that the ARCIC process will begin again,' he told me. 'The Pontifical Council for Promoting Christian Unity is clearly committed to doing what it can for the process, and if we go into issues about the local and universal Church, even though [Pope

Benedict] has made his own commitments on that pretty clear, I think he'll be supportive of our discussion.'

* * *

Liturgy was the subject of a major internal dispute from the late 1990s onwards, as Rome set about reclaiming control of the translation of texts, a task delegated to local Churches after Vatican II. In the Vatican, liturgical matters are the responsibility of the Congregation for Divine Worship and the Sacraments (CDW) and not, therefore, under direct CDF oversight. But Ratzinger is acknowledged by friend and critic alike to have played a key part in this process: further evidence of his very high status. Also at the root of this episode is his command of the subject. He probably knows and cares more about it than any Pope for many centuries. During the late 1990s, he devoted part of his summer holiday each year to writing *The Spirit of the Liturgy*,[14] a work pregnant with indicators of the ways in which worship might evolve during his papacy.

First among these signs is his insistence (a reverberation of sentiments expressed in *Milestones* and of the Eastern Orthodox perspective) that liturgy is grounded in revelation. This contrasts with the opinion of many Western experts that no liturgical text is divinely inspired, and therefore valid for all times and cultures. On this view, even the greatest texts of the Mass have achieved their status only through a combination of their intrinsic merits and historical accident. An implication of Ratzinger's contention is that Christianity forms its own culture: it can be introduced into non-European societies without concessions to local custom. Accordingly, he takes a dim view of innovations such as liturgical dance and the use of what he terms 'Dionysiac' or 'irrational' ingredients such as rock music in worship. This in turn is queried on assorted grounds by those who see language and other channels of religious truth as by definition provisional.

Ratzinger's high view of liturgy rests partly on the idea that Christian worship originates in the Cleansing of the Temple. Like some other commentators, he sees a very developed (that is, orthodox) incarnational doctrine implied by this and other gospel episodes in which Jesus appears to locate the new Temple in his own person. Second, the Cardinal expresses a preference for the eastward position (a literal 'orientation'), arguing that too much attention is focused on priests when they celebrate Mass facing the people. He views this post-conciliar development as a deviation, and likens the reform of the liturgy as a whole to an uncovered fresco that is now endangered by environmental factors.

Historically, priests faced east (with their backs to the congregation) during the Eucharist because east is the direction both of Jerusalem and of the rising sun. But evidence suggests that the westward position was not unknown in the ancient Church, and the authors of *Sacrosanctum Concilium* plainly thought that they were recovering a sense of the Mass as a communal celebration of the Passion and resurrection. This prompted the tart suggestion from some reviewers of *The Spirit of the Liturgy* that Ratzinger was also unhappy with parts of the fresco itself.[15] For our purposes, it is sufficient to note some of the Cardinal's activities, and to give an idea of the sheer strength of his feelings. As Prefect, he developed warm relations with Le Barroux Abbey in southern France, a centre of Tridentine worship, and sometimes attended meetings at Wigratzbad in Bavaria, where former Lefebvrists reconciled to the Catholic Church have a seminary.

The following passage, possibly the most passionately expressed part of *God and the World*, gives a further taste of his feelings:

> For fostering a true consciousness in liturgical matters, it is also important that the proscription against the form of liturgy in valid use up to 1970 should be lifted. Anyone who nowadays advocates the continuing existence of [the Tridentine] liturgy or takes part in it is treated like a leper; all tolerance ends here. There has never been anything like this in history; in doing this we are despising and proscribing the Church's whole past. How can one trust her present if things are that way? I must say, quite openly, that I don't understand why so many of my episcopal brethren have to a great extent submitted to this rule of intolerance, which for no apparent reason is opposed to making the necessary inner reconciliations within the Church.[16]

Such comments had practical ramifications long before Ratzinger's election as Pope. The clampdown on liturgical commissions during recent years has been firmest in the English-speaking world, viewed with reason by Rome as a laboratory for linguistic experiments reflecting social changes such as the higher profile of feminism. English poses additional problems for translators. Its vocabulary is larger, and its registers broader, than those of French, Spanish and Italian, for example. Nor is inclusive language much of a dilemma outside the anglophone world.

For a map and compass through this difficult field, it is necessary once again to revisit the provisions of Vatican II. *Sacrosanctum Concilium* ordained that normative texts in Latin for all Western rites would be produced by the CDW. These were to be rendered in the vernacular under the auspices of episcopal conferences, or, where several countries shared the same language, by joint bodies producing common versions. For the 26 Houses of Bishops in the anglophone world, this task was executed by the International Commission on English in the Liturgy (ICEL). From the late 1960s onwards, ICEL was charged with presenting translated texts to the various bishops' conferences, which were free to accept or reject them. If they received requisite two-thirds majorities at national levels, these translations were forwarded for final approval in Rome. A guide to the principles of translation known by its French title, *Comme le prévoit*, was published in 1969.

The entire corpus of Roman liturgy was recast and reissued in Latin during the decade after Vatican II, and ICEL had produced vernacular translations by the late 1970s. The verdict on this project has been mixed. Ratzinger, as we have seen, believes the loss of the old liturgy to have been a disaster, and has even ascribed declining church attendance to distaste for the new rite. In English-speaking countries, many simply feel that the new Mass (in use since 1973) is mundane, and based on a poorly judged preference for accessibility over quality. Those of a more theological bent also detect the scent of Pelagianism (over-emphasising unaided human resources, and downplaying the paramountcy of divine grace) in the first generation of vernacular liturgy. Traditionalists cite many examples of this, including the offertory prayer of the Seventh Sunday in Ordinary Time. The Latin version reads: '*Mysteria tua, Domine, debitis servitiis exsequentes, supplices te rogamus, ut, quod ad honorem tuae maiestatis offerimus, nobis proficiat ad salutem.*' A literal translation might run as follows: 'As in our due service we perform your mysteries, O Lord, we humbly ask you that what we offer to the honour of your majesty may help us to salvation.' But the 1973 ICEL version is 'Lord, as we make this offering, may our worship in Spirit and in truth bring us to salvation.'

Fergus Kerr's critical essay on *The Ratzinger Report*, discussed in Chapter 6, also rides to the Cardinal's defence in a scathing comment on ICEL's rendering of this prayer. 'Of course this is a "re-creation", not a literal translation,' Kerr writes.

> But God is not asked for anything, humbly or otherwise, in the ICEL version. It is 'our worship', rather than 'what we offer', that is presented as bringing salvation. It is our worship 'in Spirit and in truth', which people as affected by 'the liberal-radical libertarian culture' as Cardinal Ratzinger (rightly) thinks many of us are would be strongly inclined to take to be some 'subjective experience', that brings us to salvation.

Here 'as so often', in Kerr's view, 'the ICEL liturgy is pervaded with some perverse determination to Pelagianise one prayer after another – not to mention the banality of so much of the language. Again and again, the accent is shifted towards *us* and our subjective attitudes, and away from Christ and the objective realities of his work for our salvation.'

In defence of ICEL, it is pointed out that the original translators were obliged to work at great speed. They also expected that their efforts would be revised after a shortish interval, in the light of experience and reflection. This process began almost straight-away, and observers describe the Commission's work during the 1980s and 90s as painstaking. Less than 50 per cent of the liturgy had been revised in second-generation translations by the turn of the millennium, but a new rite for the Eucharist, *Roman Missal: Sacramentary*, begun in 1982, had been approved by a large majority of English-speaking bishops by 1997.

ICEL members certainly believed that they had taken due note of the criticisms. Reflecting on this process,[17] Fr Chris Walsh, a British liturgist, has written that the first-generation translations were right to avoid sixteenth-century liturgical English, 'just when its hereditary custodian the Anglican Communion was in the process of abandoning it', and the 'mannered pastiche' of unofficial Catholic prayer books in use before Vatican II.

> However, it may freely be admitted that the spare and very basic English [which ICEL initially] settled for has proved

unequal to the demands of a richer language that should be formal without being elitist, accessible without being colloquial, sonorous and rhythmic, nourishing and memorable, rich in allusion and imagery, challenging and suggestive enough to bear regular repetition. We would like to think that the 'second-generation' texts, particularly the Sacramentary, have come much closer to the ideal.

Two examples help bear out this argument. One of the collects for Easter Day reads as follows in Latin:

Deus, qui hodierna die, per Unigenitum tuum, aeternitatis nobis aditum, devicta morte, reserasti, da nobis, quaesumus, ut, qui resurrectionis dominicae sollemnia colimus, per innovationem tui Spiritus in lumine vitae resurgamus.

The 1973 translation of this reads

God our Father, by raising Christ your Son you conquered the power of death and opened for us the way to eternal life. Let our celebration today raise us up and renew our lives by the Spirit that is within us.

ICEL's 1998 version is more stringent:

On this most holy day, Lord God, through the triumph of your only-begotten Son you have shattered the gates of death and opened the way to everlasting life. Grant, we beseech you, that we who celebrate the festival of the Lord's resurrection may rise to a new and glorious life through the quickening power of your Spirit.

Another apt example comes from a collect for the Twenty-First Sunday in Ordinary Time:

Deus, qui fidelium mentes unius efficis voluntatis, da populis tuis id amare quod praecipis, id desiderare quod promittis, ut, inter mundanas varietates, ibi nostra fixa sint corda, ubi vera sunt gaudia.

In 1973, this was rendered as

Father, help us to seek the values that will bring us enduring joy in this changing world. In our desire for what you promise make us one in mind and heart.

The proposed 1998 revision was

O God, you inspire the hearts of the faithful with a single longing. Grant that your people may love what you command and desire what you promise, so that, amid the uncertain things of this world, our hearts may be fixed where true joys are found.

Behind Walsh's comment quoted above lies a substantial theoretical debate. There are two broad schools of thought on the reminting of seminal texts composed in the remote past. In one, described by the biblical expert Eugene Nida as dynamic-equivalence translation, entire sentences are reconceived as if written in normal modern English, with subordinate clauses and avoidance of repetition. Others, though (including Robert Alter, another distinguished voice), believe that this approach is based on a misunderstanding of literary translation. For him, the translator's job is not to make the reader believe that the text was written in normal modern English in the first place, but to suggest the flavour of the original language; and this can be achieved only by a measure of imitation and by refusing to gloss the meaning of the original through paraphrase.

ICEL opted for dynamic equivalence, and Walsh enlists the support of Hilaire Belloc, for whom the essence of translation is 'the resurrection of an alien thing in a native body, not the dressing of it up in native clothes but the giving to it of native flesh and blood'. The use of inclusive language (much more of an issue for second- than first-generation ICEL translators, given the evolving social climate) evidently formed an important ingredient of this approach. In brief, the strategy was to use non-gender-specific terms in so-called horizontal contexts, that is, when referring to human beings and the liturgical assembly. References to God (the vertical dimension) were to respect the givenness of revelation, but also, in Walsh's words, 'to avoid the gratuitous use of male pronouns and imagery not demanded by the original, and where possible and appropriate to recover biblically-based female imagery'.

This was judged unacceptable in Rome. In 1996, Ratzinger's old friend Jorge Medina Estévez became Prefect of the CDW and quickly turned down ICEL's draft ordination rite. Matters deteriorated thereafter, and the Congregation eventually rejected the new Missal in 2001. Given Ratzinger's volleys in *Milestones* and *God and the World*, it is easy to guess the cardinals' joint view. In letters to ICEL staff, Medina rejected dynamic-equivalence translation in favour of formal correspondence, even extending to punctuation and capitalisation. The new prescriptions were codified in *Liturgiam Authenticam*, a CDW Instruction published in May 2001 without the prior knowledge of bishops' conferences. Several months later, the Vatican distributed a new standard Latin edition of the *Missale Romanum*, designed to serve as a basis for all future translations. (Its general introduction contains a sharp warning about the putative decline of due reverence in church, and an order that priests should no longer leave the sanctuary at the exchange of the peace.)

These developments met with a quizzical public verdict from several ICEL members, and heavy private censure of Medina, whose grasp of the questions at stake was limited by his poor English. Against this background, the CDW established a committee called *Vox Clara* (Clear Voice) in 2002 to oversee ICEL's work. It consisted of 12 English-speaking prelates from nine countries under the chairmanship of Archbishop George Pell of Sydney. In August of that year, the chairman of ICEL's episcopal board, Bishop Maurice Taylor of Galloway, in Scotland, and Dr John Page, an American scholar who had been ICEL's executive secretary for 22 years, both stood down from the Commission. Their respective posts were filled by Bishop Arthur Roche and Fr Bruce Harbert, both from Britain. In a statement on the turn of events, Taylor said that 'many good people connected with ICEL [had] suffered' during the previous few years. 'The members of ICEL's Episcopal Board have in effect been judged to be irresponsible in the liturgical texts that they have approved . . . And the labours of all those faithful and dedicated priests, religious, and laypeople who devoted many hours of their lives to the work of ICEL have been called into question.' Taylor's conclusion does not need decoding. The impression had been given, 'and indeed is seemingly fostered by some, that ICEL is a recalcitrant group of people, uncooperative, even disobedient. This is mistaken and untrue.'

In October 2003, Harbert, Roche, Cardinal Francis Arinze (Medina's successor as Prefect of the CDW) and the presidents of English-speaking bishops' conferences met. On this occasion, relief was expressed that an atmosphere of confrontation had apparently given way to greater concord, and another revised Missal, then in the early stages of preparation, was discussed. Detailed forecasts about the shape of the embryonic liturgy would be premature, however. A draft of a new translation of the Mass was circulated to bishops' conferences in January 2004: as expected, the document sometimes sounds mannered to many English-speaking ears, and inclusive language is largely dropped. But this version is likely to be reworked in what promises to be a lengthy revision process. The first-generation Missal will probably remain in use for some years yet.

What other factors were in play during this unhappy episode? ICEL certainly had influential opponents. Some scholars in the field thought that even its second-generation team of translators was too swayed by political correctness, and other critics judged that its procedures were unduly cumbersome. Medina's actions partly arose from complaints of American bishops, who felt strong-armed into all-or-nothing acceptance of ICEL texts without the chance to tweak them. There was also consternation among traditionalists when certain new translations were used liturgically before they had been fully authorised. (Examples include a new psalter employed unofficially in parts of the American Church during the 1990s.) ICEL's defenders are unrepentant. 'Yes, we chanced our arm on occasion', one former member of the Commission told me.

> But I don't think the trial use of those psalms in church was such a terrible thing. If you have a new lawnmower you want to try it out, not leave it in the garage. More generally, I think that the minority of Americans who complained to Rome did so because they had lost the argument on the floor of their own House of Bishops.

That non-anglophone liturgists were also targeted by Vatican officials can be illustrated by two brief examples. During the 1990s, the Japanese and Korean liturgical commissions were admonished for their allegedly faulty vernacular translations. But no one at the CDW spoke either of the two languages concerned.

It emerged that the Congregation's officials had asked Japanese and Korean seminarians in Rome whether the new texts were literal translations of the Latin. The answer, predictably, was no: deep-seated differences between Oriental and Western languages make such correspondence almost unachievable. Bishops in the two countries concerned were angered by what they saw as an affront to their authority.

Another anecdote fills out the picture. In November 2003, a conference was held at the Benedictine college of Sant'Anselmo in Rome, a centre for liturgical research, to mark the fortieth anniversary of *Sacrosanctum Concilium*. One of the addresses was given by a Spanish scholar, Fr Ignacio Calabuig. Turning to Cardinal Arinze (a Nigerian without specialist expertise on liturgy), he said: 'I must tell the Prefect that the devastating impression the Congregation seems to be spreading, that people of great culture in their own lands are not capable of translating liturgical texts into their own mother tongue, is causing great discontent and concern in the Church.' The 600-strong audience applauded for so long that Arinze eventually joined in.

The wider lesson drawn by Chris Walsh from such episodes is that liturgy has formed another major strand in John Paul and Ratzinger's restorationist programme. Vatican II had redressed the terms of the Council of Trent by cautiously returning the '*jus liturgicum*' to bishops' conferences: this provided scope for regional variations, cultural adaptations and organic development. But Walsh thinks that the ship has changed direction.

> Many would fear that policy-makers in Rome today, egged on by a discontented constituency in several countries, are attempting to redress the balance again: to restrict the prerogatives of bishops and bishops' conferences, to slow down or halt altogether the process of adaptation and inculturation, to establish hands-on control and micro-management even of the vernacular liturgies, in defence of the 'substantial unity of the Roman rite' which they would see as imperilled if not already shattered.

He concludes the article already cited by suggesting that 'whatever one may think of the validity of their concerns, we are experiencing a manifest breakdown of two fundamental ecclesiological principles, collegiality and subsidiarity.'

8

The German Shepherd

If the evidence of the past three chapters proves Ratzinger's pre-eminence during John Paul's papacy, it also helps to explain why he was regarded in some quarters as unsuited for the highest office. The Pope's declining health formed a source of limitless speculation among Vatican watchers for over a decade, as he succumbed to the effects of Parkinson's disease. His growing physical incapacity was obvious from 1994, and hair-raising tales of his mental degeneration emerged during the three years before his death.[1] So the reign with which Ratzinger was so closely identified could not last long beyond the turn of the millennium. John Paul had asked the Prefect to remain in post for a further five years in 1991 and 1996; this request was again repeated in 2001. Declining a further offer of resignation in April 2002 (a ritual matter connected with Ratzinger's seventy-fifth birthday), John Paul also realised that the hands of his successor might be tied if he were to inherit a recently installed head of the CDF.

The Cardinal himself let it be known that he wished for nothing more than to retire at the appropriate moment to Pentling, be near Georg once more, and devote his remaining strength to theology. Nor was his own health very good. He suffered two strokes – one during the early 1990s, another a decade later – which weakened his eyesight and heart. During the first, he fell over and lay unconscious for some time before the alarm was raised. Ratzinger never recovered fully from these episodes. Photos of him taken in recent years (especially the informal shots shown to me by one of his friends) show a shrivelled and weary-looking figure.

Critics saw plenty more evidence that suggested he was not a serious contender for the papacy. He was a scholar-bureaucrat, not a pastor, with a mixed record at running a diocese. He lacked John Paul's presence and his talent for working a crowd. For reasons already explored, he seemed ill at ease with non-European cultures, despite the growing importance of Third World voices in the councils of the Church. (As one Roman observer suggested to me, 'even with African and Asian bishops, let alone humbler members of their flocks, he has sometimes seemed like a fish out of water.') The tag about his being player as well as referee was applied again. It meant that he was still seen as divisive.

Though these reservations are serious, they reveal as much about the critics as about their apparent target. Almost all the cardinals entitled to vote for a new Pope had been appointed by John Paul, and most were in their seventies. Few possessed great charisma. What from one point of view seemed to be Ratzinger's weaknesses looked like strengths in a different light. Many electors did not want another long papacy, for instance; so age was not necessarily a handicap. And the Prefect's insider status had earned him many admirers as well as enemies. It is probably fair to suggest that from the early 1990s, major matters of church government were in the hands of a triumvirate consisting of John Paul, Ratzinger and Sodano, with the Secretary of State handling temporal affairs, and the Prefect overseeing disciplinary matters. Though alarming to some, this fed the sense in many quarters that Ratzinger was a safe pair of hands. It also gave him a high brand-recognition factor. He had met and dealt with all his brother cardinals at some point, and was probably the only figure in the conclave who could name everyone else without a stumble. (Many other electors were virtual strangers to one another, and monolingual.) A further point had long been made, but its implications became clear only with hindsight. The energies of the Pope and his enforcer were channelled in different ways. John Paul achieved some great things by focusing on the big picture. He took the Christian message to a larger audience than anyone else in history, played a leading part in the overthrow of Soviet Communism, and was the prime instigator of international efforts to cancel Third World debt. But he was bored by administration. When challenged once by Cardinal Arns of Brazil about curial reform, he answered that it would be a task for his successor. It was this attitude, according to onlookers across the spectrum, that was responsible for the sometimes uncoordinated quality of Vatican operations. 'Reform' of the Curia could thus mean different things. Many cardinals wary about liberalisation may nevertheless have wanted a candidate with more time for nuts and bolts. It should also be said that some traditionalists (Ratzinger among them, one suspects) who admired John Paul were nonetheless put off by the cult of personality that he encouraged. They welcomed the prospect of a less high-profile successor.

The first weeks of 2005 saw a new outbreak of medical prognostications about the ailing Pope. On Sunday 30 January, he gave his usual address and blessing from the window of his study, and was seen to laugh as a peace dove he'd released flew back into the room. But on the Tuesday, he was taken by ambulance to the Gemelli hospital, near the Vatican, with respiratory problems afterwards diagnosed as acute laryngeal tracheitis. His face a mask, the Pope was wheeled to the window of his room on Sunday 6 February, and managed to recite a part of the Angelus. A message to the crowd assembled outside was read by Sodano's deputy, Archbishop Leonardo Sandri.

Against medical advice, John Paul returned to the Vatican on 10 February, travelling by popemobile in a slow procession. Thousands turned out to greet him in the Via Gregorio VII and other streets near St Peter's. But he was back in hospital a fortnight later with further breathing difficulties. His consent was sought for a tracheotomy – an incision in the passage carrying air from the larynx to the windpipe. The life-saving procedure went ahead, leaving the Pontiff barely able to speak. On 1 March, he nevertheless received a visit from Ratzinger, and the two talked briefly in Italian and German. Forty-eight hours on, the Pope's long-serving press spokesman, Joaquín Navarro-Valls, spoke of the patient's 'continual' improvement. He left hospital for a second time on 13 March, and was only seen in public on a handful of further occasions before his death on 2 April. These included a poignant appearance on Easter Day, during which he tried but failed to pronounce a blessing *urbi et orbi*. Some medical commentators insisted that his condition was not immediately life-threatening, but changed their minds by the middle of the week on hearing that the Pope had endured cardio-circulatory collapse and septic shock. He received the last rites during the evening of Thursday 31 March, and died just after 9.30 p.m. two days later.

Familiar interregnum rituals – supplemented by a detailed guide to procedure produced in 1996 – now took effect. John Paul's body was at first placed in the Vatican's Clementine Hall, usually used for audiences, and then carried in procession to St Peter's. About five million mourners turned out to pay their respects: the space around the basilica held a human river fed by numberless tributaries. Though the spectacle was mocked in some quarters (there were Protestants and non-believers who felt their allegiances confirmed), it was generally short on cheap emotion. Many waited patiently for up to 24 hours for a sight of the man they cherished, even if they hadn't always agreed with him.

As Dean of the Sacred College, a post to which he had been elected by a small group of senior cardinals in 2001, Ratzinger now took a leading part in coordinating events. His masterly performances at this time are widely seen as pivotal to his election as Pope. He chaired the cardinals' 13 meetings (termed General Congregations) that took place between 2 April and the opening of the conclave 16 days later, and presided at John Paul's funeral on the 8th. Preaching at such an event demanded a mixture of gravitas and savvy. Scores of heads of state and government had come, but part of the 500,000-strong congregation was boisterous. Ratzinger's homily was well judged in content, and well delivered. He gauged his timing to allow for regular applause, and cries of *'santo subito!'*, reflecting demands for John Paul's speedy canonisation. He described the late Pope's appointment as auxiliary bishop in Krakow as the start of a venture in self-sacrifice. Leaving the academic world, 'leaving this challenging engagement with young people, leaving the great intellectual endeavour of striving to understand and interpret the mystery of that creature which is man' – all this 'must have seemed to him like losing his very self . . .'. But Karol Wojtyla had gained his life by losing it.

> Our Pope . . . never wanted to make his own life secure, to keep it for himself. He wanted to give of himself unreservedly, to the very last moment, for Christ and thus also for us. And therefore he came to experience how everything which he had given over into the Lord's hands came back to him in a new way. His love of words, of poetry, of literature, became an essential part of his pastoral mission and gave new vitality, new urgency, new attractiveness to the preaching of the gospel even when it is a sign of contradiction.

Ratzinger ended with a flourish: 'We can be sure that our beloved Pope is standing today at the window of the Father's house, that he sees us and blesses us.' Eyebrows were raised in some theological circles, because of the implication that John Paul was already in heaven. But the multitude loved it. The ceremony also provided a chance to cast an eye over the other cardinals, many of whom looked wisplike in the gusty conditions. Wind almost blew off the chasuble of Cardinal Carlo Maria Martini, emeritus Archbishop of Milan. Often described as a likely future Pope during the 1990s, he was himself struck by Parkinson's disease before his retirement in 2002, and has since spent long periods in hospital.

On 9 April, the church authorities imposed a news blackout in a foretaste of the greater secrecy of the conclave. Though this indicates that commentators should be cautious about speculating – cardinal-electors swear an oath not to disclose voting details – the restrictions cannot be taken at face value. Events at the past few conclaves have been reliably pieced together, partly because some cardinals over the age of 80 contribute to the process informally. They have no oath to break, and may not feel coy about briefing journalists or others with press links. Pundits who had done the clerical equivalent of talking to a man who'd talked to a girl were announcing by the middle of the week beginning 11 April that between 30 and 50 cardinals had already declared for Ratzinger. This intelligence was probably right; but it also showed what an inexact science Vaticanology can be. The obvious implications of the news were immediately discounted in a BBC Radio 4 programme on the conclave by three well-known religious affairs correspondents. The front-runner would quickly peak and then give way to a younger and less controversial contender, they assured listeners. Among their tips (shared by a cross-section of apparently well-informed opinion) were Dionigi Tettamanzi of Milan, Angelo Scola of Venice, Jorge Bergoglio of Buenos Aires, Ivan Dias of Mumbai, and Cláudio Hummes of Sao Paulo.

John Paul's blueprint for procedure before and during the election had included construction of a handsome residence, the Casa Santa Marta, inside the Vatican walls to house about one hundred and thirty people. (Electors at previous conclaves had frequently suffered discomfort in makeshift apartments near the Sistine Chapel.) The 115 cardinals with voting rights were next seen together in St Peter's on Monday 18 April for the Mass *pro eligendo papa*. Ratzinger was again the *ex officio* preacher, and this time he struck a more familiar note. Contemporary Christians are often at sea without an anchor:

> tossed from one extreme to the other; from Marxism to liberalism, from collectivism to radical individualism; from atheism to a vague religious mysticism; from agnosticism to syncretism and so on. Every day new sects are born, and what St Paul said about the deception of humanity is demonstrated, about the craftiness that tends to lead to error. To have a clear faith, according to the creed of the Church, is often styled as fundamentalism. Meanwhile, relativism . . . appears as the only attitude suited to modern times. [This] recognises nothing as definitive, and . . . regards one's self and one's own desires as the final measure . . .

The fruit that lasts, he added, was 'what we have planted in peoples' souls – love, understanding; the gesture capable of touching hearts; the word that opens the soul to the joy of the Lord'.

These words got less favourable notices. While some believed that the Dean of the College had every right to speak the truth as he saw it, others thought the address revealed partisanship, even a thirst for power. A plausible alternative explanation is that it showed the complexity of clerical ambition. No level-headed person, especially no one of 78 in indifferent health, would welcome the exceptional burdens of papal office. On the other hand, Ratzinger was certainly keen to perpetuate the model of the Church he had shaped with John Paul. It was a vision shared by a large proportion of the other electors, all but two of whom were John Paul's appointees. Looking back, it seems to have been fanciful to imagine that they would bite a hand that had fed them.

The cardinals gathered at 4.30 p.m. and processed into the Sistine Chapel, passing two stoves on their left used for burning counted ballot papers, and taking their places at 12 tables, placed in two rows of three on either side of the aisle. Near the altar, under Michelangelo's fresco of the Last Judgement, stood an urn in which votes were to be deposited. An inconclusive outcome of the first two ballots was inconclusively signalled when grey smoke emerged from the chimney of the Sistine Chapel at 8 p.m. Then the fumes turned black. Ratzinger is believed to have received about forty votes in the first ballot, thereby confirming the rumours that had circulated the previous week. Yet it was still possible that this support would ebb. Its solidity became incontrovertible only after the third ballot, held the following morning, when the front-runner apparently scored higher than fifty. This left him strongly placed to garner about two dozen more votes (he needed 77) to win the necessary two-thirds majority: other fancied contenders were flagging, and a new rule introduced by John Paul stated that prolonged deadlock could be broken after seven days if a candidate had a simple majority.

Some saw signs of a split reflected in the appearance of black smoke above the chapel at noon the following day. The misconception was soon dispelled. It is customary for voters to fall behind the top-scoring cardinal in a gesture of unity, and when the electors returned to the chapel after lunch for the fourth ballot, Ratzinger knew that the highest dignity would almost certainly be his. John Allen of the *National Catholic Reporter* is among several correspondents to have estimated that he had almost one hundred supporters.[2] Applause broke out when the future Pope notched up 77 votes, though he himself looked 'rather sad', according to Cardinal Meisner.

It was then for the Sub-Dean of the College, Cardinal Sodano, to ask the latest Bishop of Rome whether he accepted his canonical election, and the name by which he was to be known. Ratzinger had had due time to prepare a response. He explained the grounds for his choice: that Benedict is the patron saint of Europe; that Benedict XV had served for a short time and suffered; and that this Pope (who reigned from 1914 to 1922) had still achieved much in the cause of peace.[3] Another concatenation of rituals supervened. Benedict XVI was greeted by the cardinals, and then led to a small vestry, known as the room of tears, to be fitted out in a white soutane. Smoke went up. Again, the crowd outside St Peter's were at first in two minds about whether it really was the *fumata bianca*. But before grey resolved into white, many bystanders knew from the time (it was just before 6 p.m.) that the suspense was almost over. If a further ballot were needed, no message would have been sent up the chimney for another hour. The authorities had let it be known that the bells of St Peter's would peal in confirmation of the smoke signal; this finally happened after a nerve-stretching delay of 20 minutes.

Crowds scurried towards the Vatican from all over central Rome. At 6.45 p.m., the outcome of the conclave was announced from the central *loggia* of St Peter's by Jorge Medina, the senior Cardinal Deacon. Departing from protocol, he greeted his 'dear brothers and sisters' in several languages, before making the customary disclosure in Latin, complete with theatrical pauses: '*Annuntio vobis gaudium magnum; Habemus Papam: Eminentissimum ac reverendissimum Dominum Josephum, Sanctae Romanae Ecclesiae Cardinalem Ratzinger, qui sibi nomen imposuit Benedictum Decimum Sextum.*' The ovation had started before Medina stopped speaking, because only one '*Josephum*' was both well known and *papabile*. (This contrasted with the momentary astonishment caused by news of John Paul II's election. '*Carolum*' was assumed to be the 85-year-old Cardinal Carlo Confalonieri.) It all had something in common with the corresponding scene in Anthony Burgess's *Earthly Powers*, one of the most colourful fictional accounts of post-conclave euphoria: 'The crowd gaudiated magnally: old ladies in black wept, teeth gleamed in stubbled faces, strangers shook hands with each other, children jumped as though Mickey Mouse were soon to come on, the horns of Roman cars rejoiced plaintively.'[4] But Burgess's novel portrays a reformer, Cardinal Carlo Campanati, who as Pope Gregory XVII transforms the institution bequeathed by Pius XII. What delighted many onlookers on 19 April 2005 was the belief that things would stay the same.

Medina retreated from view as Vatican staff unfurled the huge maroon papal banner. Benedict then came out with arms aloft, revealing the sleeves of a black jumper. He'd had a cold, and needed an extra layer to ward off the spring chill. 'After the great Pope John Paul II,' he declared, his timbre more emphatic and a little higher than usual, 'the cardinals have elected me, a humble servant in the vineyard of the Lord . . .' Then he retreated for a champagne supper with the cardinals in the Casa Santa Marta. A few days later, the Pope painted the following picture of his election to a group of German pilgrims: 'As slowly the balloting showed me, so to speak, that the guillotine would fall on me, I got quite dizzy. So with deep conviction, I told the Lord: "Don't do this to me! You have younger and better men . . ." This time, he didn't listen . . .'

* * *

American reaction was typical of responses elsewhere. Among politicians, President George W. Bush called Benedict 'a man of great wisdom and knowledge'. The Archbishop of Philadelphia, Cardinal Justin Rigali, described the Pope as 'very serene', and forecast that ecumenism, interfaith dialogue and the cause of social justice would all prosper on his watch. The Archbishop of Detroit, Cardinal Adam Maida, said that 'with all of his gifts and talents, and even some of his shortcomings', the Pope would 'somehow be able to reach others'. By contrast, Professor Thomas Groome of Boston College was reported as commenting that only 5 per cent of American Catholics would welcome the result of the election. 'Some of us are bewildered by it, disappointed,' he said.[5] In the UK, a *Tablet* editorial two days later was a compound of views. Benedict's diagnosis of Europe's spiritual ills had much to commend it, but there was 'also a danger of being so aggressive in arguing against Europe's post-modern culture that the very opposition the Church is trying to overcome is in fact stimulated . . . It would be a crucial mistake for him to assume that theologians on the more progressive wing of the church are somehow part of a fifth column trying to undermine it.'[6]

Others were still reflecting on the electoral process itself. It is widely thought that Cardinal Martini scored highly in the first ballot before insisting his candidacy was unviable. Whether this supposition is correct or not, it seems clear that the forces of reform were not strong, either organisationally or numerically. 'Votes for candidates other than Ratzinger and Martini were apparently spread thinly between about twelve others,' according to a well-informed observer who did not want to be named. 'Tettamanzi, for example, who was widely tipped as a possible victor before the conclave, is said only to have received two votes in the first ballot.' If this version of events is broadly accurate, my source added,

> you have, from the Monday evening onwards, a man who already has slightly more than half the votes he needs to be elected Pope, and no other candidate with more than a handful of backers. Now it is obvious that quite a few cardinals did not wish to elect Ratzinger. But whether Martini's candidacy collapsed in the way some believe or not, there was no other horse within sight of the leader. Vatican cardinals wanted to choose someone whose ecclesiology would not threaten the

immense power over the life of the Church which the Roman Curia has acquired, for the first time in Catholic history, over the past 130 years. They got their way. In Joseph Ratzinger they had a scholar of undoubted eminence, a good man exhibiting simplicity and saintliness of life, whose model of church government suited their purposes.

The new Pope's inaugural Mass took place on the following Sunday. He wanted the ceremony to be in St Peter's, on the grounds that its architecture focuses attention on Christ rather than the Pope, but agreed to move out of doors as a concession to the crowds. More than 100,000 came from Germany alone. Having prayed first at the tomb of Peter, the Pontiff emerged into the sunshine; he was vested in gold, his mitre and chasuble emblazoned with images of shells. At the ceremonial climax of the service, he was presented with the so-called fisherman's ring (imprinted with a boat) and his pallium. This scarf-like woollen garment, which is given to all metropolitan archbishops by the reigning Pope, had been redesigned to match a patristic style, and included a long appendage hanging from Benedict's left shoulder. Many liked it, but some thought this pallium a high-maintenance affair (Archbishop Piero Marini, the papal Master of Ceremonies, straightened it several times), which made the papal garb stand out unduly. Recently appointed archbishops have received the pallium in its conventional form.

The homily was vintage Ratzinger: tight but accessible, intelligent, memorably phrased. It is worth quoting at some length. He began with a greeting to all the baptised, as well as to Roman Catholics; to the Jewish people, with whom 'we are joined by a great spiritual heritage'; and 'to all men and women of today, to believers and non-believers alike'. It was not the moment to state his programme, the Pope continued. He would instead confine himself to comment on the gospel symbols, sheep and fish respectively, represented by his pallium and ring. Rulers in ancient Near-Eastern societies were also referred to as shepherds of their sheep, but only because the animal was considered disposable. By emphasising the sheep's infinite value, and the cost to the shepherd in rescuing it, Jesus had overturned conventional assumptions.

Benedict then itemised the deserts in which contemporary humanity was lost: 'There is the desert of poverty, the desert of hunger and thirst, the desert of abandonment, of loneliness, of destroyed love. There is the desert of God's darkness, the emptiness of souls no longer aware of their dignity or the goal of human life.' The world's physical deserts were growing, he said, because the internal deserts had become so vast. 'Therefore the earth's treasures no longer serve to build God's garden for all to live in, but they have been made to serve the powers of exploitation and destruction. The Church as a whole and all her pastors . . . must . . . lead people out of the desert towards the place of life.' He asked for the prayers of his flock to make him strong in the face of contemporary 'wolves'.

Though also used by Jesus, the image of the fisherman is less neat. Rescue benefits a lost sheep, but aquatic creatures do not benefit from being hauled up in nets. Benedict adopted the traditional image of the sea as the worldly peril from which Christians seek deliverance: 'the net of the gospel pulls us out of the waters of death and brings us into the splendour of God's light, into true life.' If this comment suggested a sombre picture of the world, Benedict went on to anticipate such a verdict by accentuating the positive: 'only when we meet the living God in Christ do we know what life is. We are not some casual and meaningless product of evolution. Each of us is the result of a thought of God. Each of us is willed, each of us is loved, each of us is necessary.' The homily drew to an end in a similar vein:

> there is nothing more beautiful than to be surprised by the gospel, by the encounter with Christ. There is nothing more beautiful than to know him and to speak to others of our friendship with him. The task of the shepherd, and the task of the fisher of men, can often seem wearisome. But it is beautiful and wonderful, because it is truly a service to joy, to God's joy, which longs to break into the world.

The Pope's footwork was approved by the feminist commentator Margaret Hebblethwaite, among others. She noted that he had 'diplomatically avoided mentioning both the first reading (Acts 4:8–12), with its phrase about Christ as a unique Saviour, that would have reignited the controversies over interfaith dialogue', and the epistle (1 Peter 5:1–5, 10–11), which calls on young people to submit to the elders. 'Instead of calling for doctrinal orthodoxy and obedience', she continued, the Pope 'had reached out to the people as "dear friends", a phrase he repeated four times.'[7]

After the Mass, Benedict boarded an open-topped jeep for a meander through the crowds. They, too, evidently liked what they saw. An eminent theologian with reservations about the former Cardinal suggested to me that he had undergone a 'Sistine Chapel conversion', while Benedict's longstanding friends said simply that his true colours had finally emerged in a more obvious way. Both verdicts seem to be true in different respects. The binary alternatives necessitated by practical decision-making (turn left or right; say yes or no) are less appropriate to the assessment of character. Cardinal Ratzinger had for long been typecast. There were good reasons for thinking the enforcer could adapt. Uniquely constraining in some respects, the papal office might also release the pastor inside the Prefect.

Benedict's hospitable instincts remained largely to the fore over the ensuing days. He met Muslim leaders on the morning after his installation, and welcomed the broadening channels of dialogue between Islam and Christianity. Later, he visited St Paul-Outside-the-Walls, one of Rome's four patriarchal basilicas, and gave an audience in the Clementine Hall to an ecumenical group of Christian leaders. Some Anglicans expressed disappointment that they were classed as members of 'ecclesial communities' rather than 'Churches' (only the Orthodox received this tribute), but there was general praise for the Pope's warmth and sense of common purpose.

The good press lasted for much of Benedict's first 100 days, and not merely because he was a new face. People were struck by his modesty – he took the triple crown traditionally worn by Popes until the 1970s off his coat of arms, and made it known that he did not wish people to kiss his ring – and by the potency of his ecumenical gestures. He has given a substantial boost to Catholic–Orthodox dialogue in collaboration with Metropolitan John Zizioulas, one of the most distinguished living theologians in the Greek Church, and underlined this in late May by going to Bari, on Italy's heel, long a frontier between the Catholic and Orthodox worlds. It has even been suggested that clerical celibacy might be reconsidered in the near future, because Ratzinger is thought to have said in private before John Paul's death that a review would be necessary during the next pontificate. Firm prophecies would be unwise at this point. Although the celibacy rule is often described as a matter of discipline rather than doctrine, this is not altogether true. A change in policy would probably also require a knock-on review of *Humanae Vitae.*

Another much-noted feature of Benedict's early period in office has been its placidity. Gone, for now, are the days of the Pope as globe-trotting evangelist and media superstar. The new Bishop of Rome underlined his diocesan role by several early visits to his cathedral, St John Lateran, and then disappeared from view for much of the summer of 2005. There have also been endearing signs of absent-mindedness. On 17 August, he greeted crowds from a balcony at Castel Gandolfo, his residence south of Rome, but forgot to bless them. Having gone back indoors, he re-emerged to correct the lapse.

A long-planned papal trip to Cologne for the Church's World Youth Day went ahead later that month, thus allowing him to visit his homeland before any other country; and his diffidence emerged in various ways at this time. As he came out of his plane, the wind blew off his skull cap, and he vacillated over whether to retrieve it. The papal entourage was transported along the Rhine to Cologne's cathedral, and Benedict addressed the crowds from his boat. 'But there was something about the Wagnerian perform-ance . . . that did not come off,' observed Robert Mickens, *The Tablet*'s Rome correspondent. 'Maybe it was the Pope's bashfulness or the fact that he was dwarfed by the distance that separated his barge from the far-off banks . . . But not even the camera close-ups helped the smiling professor-Pope play a scene so much more clearly orchestrated for his titanic and telegenic predecessor.'[8] The trip was nevertheless notable for Benedict's very warm encounters with Jews and Muslims, and his avoidance of conten-tious issues (a surprise to some, after his earlier quarrels with German Catholics) during his addresses to over 800,000 young people.

*   *   *

Do such observations suggest that revolution is round the corner? Almost certainly not. It is possible that conservatives will be disappointed, and liberals surprised, by what lies ahead; but reflection suggests that the dust will settle, not be swept away. The liturgical clampdown is plainly set to continue (if anything, Catholics can expect accelerated conservative reforms in this area), with all that it implies about the status of the local Church.

Archbishop Sean O'Malley of Boston provoked derision when he asked Rome for leave to wash the feet of women, as well as men, on Maundy Thursday in 2004: mixed groups take part in the foot-washing ritual throughout the Catholic world. His antagonists said that O'Malley and other bishops were helping to diminish their office. But episcopal timidity of this kind has its roots in the encroachments of Rome.

Official attitudes towards women also seem unlikely to change. In August 2004, the CDF published the letter 'Collaboration of Men and Women in the Church'. Although the document makes only one explicit reference to feminism, critics described its tone as implicitly anti-feminist. The letter's title bears little relation to its content, which says nothing significant about men or about collaboration. It implies that feminism is responsible for creating antagonism between the sexes, but makes no reference to the culture of male domination and violence against women which has flourished as much in the Church as in any other sector of society. The letter also offers an unassertive version of femininity based on Mary's 'dispositions of listening, welcoming, humility, faithfulness, praise and waiting'.

Dr Tina Beattie of Roehampton University, London, spoke for many Catholic feminists in voicing disappointment about this document. In an interview with me, she applauded Benedict's close friendship with Ingrid Stampa (who now lives in the papal apartment), and suggested that it might be unprecedented for a woman to occupy such a position of influence and trust in a Pope's inner circle. But Beattie still feels strong concern about the drift of church teaching on women. 'Despite his sexual conservatism,' she says,

John Paul II respected women's desire for greater equality, and several women were promoted to senior Vatican positions during the latter years of his papacy. It remains to be seen what Benedict XVI will do with this legacy, and he may yet surprise us. However, if he does not show himself capable of engaging with the signs of the times as far as women are concerned, it seems quite likely that there will continue to be a significant drift of women away from the Church – and that also means the loss of a generation of children whose mothers may not want to subject them to the anachronisms of a regressive and exclusively male religious hierarchy.

When the post-conclave exultation had levelled off, further memories of the Ratzinger style were jogged by the resignation of Fr Thomas Reese SJ as Editor of the New York-based weekly *America*. Reese had been feeling the heat of CDF disapproval for almost half of his seven-year stint in charge of the magazine. He jumped before he was pushed in early May, having hung on during the interregnum, and then concluded that his fate would be sealed by the new Pope. 'It is clear that the person who was not pleased with Tom Reese was Cardinal Ratzinger,' according to Fr José de Vera, a spokesmen at the Jesuit headquarters in Rome.[9] Other sources said that the order had supported Reese as far as possible, but would soon have faced irresistible pressure to oust him.

The problem, as usual, concerned the limits of diversity. Can a Catholic paper, owned by an arm of the Church, also provide space for dissenting views? Or must it always defend official teaching and rebut the opposition? Reese felt that loyalty to Rome ranked below a balance of opinion on the scale of editorial virtues. Conservative contributors were not turned away. An article by Ratzinger himself was published in 2001. But Reese did not shrink from carrying pieces exploring the possible authorisation of condoms to fight HIV infection; on homosexuality in the priesthood; and an article challenging the denial of communion to Catholic politicians who vote against the direction of their bishops. (Debate on this subject reached a pitch during the 2004 American presidential race, when Senator John Kerry's pro-choice stance was condemned in Rome, as well as on the campaign trail.) Reese was also responsible for an editorial comment alleging lack of due process in CDF procedures.

Negative judgements of this kind were unendurable for the Vatican. Reese was never contacted directly: following its usual drill, the CDF dealt with the Superior-General of the Jesuits, Fr Peter-Hans Kolvenbach, who then contacted the Editor's Provincial. According to de Vera, Ratzinger demanded Reese's sacking in 2004, and threatened to impose an editorial board, consisting of three bishops, to censor the magazine's contents. The row had then been defused by the intervention of powerful Jesuits with the ear of Rome, such as Cardinal Avery Dulles, but Reese realised that this was no more than a stay of execution. His instinct was confirmed when Ratzinger again sought his removal a few weeks before John Paul's death.

The wisdom of Reese's decision to bow out is further

corroborated by Benedict's choice of his own successor as Prefect. Some thought that the appointment of Walter Kasper would be an imaginative bridge-building gesture; others, aware of the implausibility of this suggestion, put their money on Cardinal Christoph Schönborn. But Schönborn's move might have disrupted the troubled Austrian Church still further. The appointment of Archbishop William Levada of San Francisco in June was an obvious token of continuity. A former junior CDF official (he served in Rome during the early 1980s), Levada was Archbishop of Portland, Oregon, from 1986 to 1995, before his translation to California. He differs from Ratzinger in that his intellectual credentials are solid rather than stellar, but theologically they are on the same page.

Several senior figures apart from Sodano (including Darío Castrillón Hoyos at the Congregation for Clergy) are due to retire fairly soon, and the form shown by their successors will be assessed keenly. But a broad prediction by Professor Nicholas Lash of Cambridge University is probably right:

> the crucial task that will have to be faced eventually, as John Quinn [emeritus Archbishop of San Francisco] and others have argued, is the transferral of executive authority, in fact and not merely in a form of words, from Pope and Curia to the College of Bishops (*sub et cum Petro*, by all means), through the establishment of some set of standing, worldwide, synodical instruments. Benedict will not face up to this challenge. It will have to be confronted by one of his successors.

A further sign that the barque of Peter had not changed course emerged in June, when the Spanish bishops, backed by the Vatican, denounced their government's plan to legalise gay marriage. About 300,000 Catholics and others later demonstrated in Madrid against the reform. There is little prospect of a meeting of minds between figures so far apart as Benedict and Spain's Prime Minister, José Luis Rodríguez Zapatero. According to one influential school of thought, the row has simply raised further questions about the legitimacy of church involvement in politics. Those who take this line tend to regard anyone expressing ambivalence about secular pluralism as authoritarian or worse. Yet as the Archbishop of Canterbury, among others, has argued, there is also something intolerant about the widespread assumption that opinions must be formed without reference to agencies or presences beyond the tangible.[10]

Ratzinger made his most sustained defence of religion's place in the public realm in his book *Church, Ecumenism and Politics*.[11] He quotes Matthew 22:21 ('render unto Caesar what is due to Caesar, and render unto God what is due to God'), suggesting that this marks an assault on the Roman sacralisation of state power and, therefore, the start of the Western idea of freedom. Aidan Nichols expounds the Cardinal's argument as follows: 'the State no longer carries a religious authority reaching into the most hidden corners of the soul. Rather does it point for its ethical foundation to an institution beyond itself.'[12] Ratzinger goes on to say that successive attempts to export Western institutional models (especially to the Islamic world) have suffered because a notion drawn from Christianity cannot always take root in other climates. 'Where there is no dualism, there is totalitarianism,' he infers. But like Williams, Ratzinger draws a striking corollary from this – that the enemies of democracy also include those engaged in a 'flight from transcendence'. Marx taught that only when humanity had come of age and jettisoned transcendence would it be possible to build a perfect world. Today, says Ratzinger, it is clearer that secular society must draw on a source of spiritual power from above. He admits that at first sight the Church seems an unlikely guide in this respect, given its past collusion in all manner of intolerance. But Christianity has also been a potent force for political good, and is all the more so today, given that its wings have been clipped by other forces.

Doubters, though, continue to question whether this process has advanced far enough. For the Spanish as for others, how the religious voice is to be modulated in conversation with other voices is not as simple a matter as it first appears. It is only partly a question of political strategy. At root, it is a theological matter: how brightly does the divine spark flicker inside those whose lifestyles and beliefs do not accord with official Catholic teaching? Is it right to distinguish sharply between grace and nature, or is the idea of 'ungraced' nature inherently flawed? We are back in the domain of *Gaudium et Spes*, the document promulgated with the full authority of an ecumenical council, but which Peter's later successor has judged to be spiritually flabby. At the start of this book, I drew on a comment of Nicholas Boyle to shed light on Bavaria's political geography. I end it by quoting his more positive verdict on *Gaudium et Spes* given during a lecture in July 2005 to mark the fortieth anniversary of the text's publication:

> we cannot spell out, either in the terms used by human wisdom, or even in the terms used by divine wisdom when it speaks with a human voice in the Church, what is Christian in the lives and beliefs of those who do not bear the name of Christ. (That surely is the true meaning of the much-abused concept of 'anonymous Christianity' – the Christianity that Christians, not non-Christians, cannot identify.) Equally, we cannot spell out what features of the new humanity being built by the secular processes of socialisation will be found again in the eternal and universal kingdom. *Gaudium et Spes'* great strength is that, by insisting on what we do not and cannot know, it finds not the fullness but the signs of God's greatness among the signs of the times.[13]

Pope Benedict does not, of course, command the content of the faith: he would be among the first to insist that he is only its trustee. But he does have a commanding role in shaping the way Christian faith is interpreted. Boyle's insight is important for this reason alone.

Notes

Introduction

1. Joseph Ratzinger, 'Free Expression and Obedience in the Church', in Hugo Rahner (ed.), *The Church: Readings in Theology* (P. J. Kenedy, 1963), p. 212.
2. The comment was made to the journalist Vittorio Messori in the interview later published in Italian as *Rapporto sulla fede*, and in English as *The Ratzinger Report* (Ignatius Press, 1985). A digest of the Italian original, translated and abridged by Elsa Iglich, Fergus Kerr OP, John Orme Mills OP and Robert Ombres OP, was published in the Dominican journal *New Blackfriars* in June 1985. All quotations from *Rapporto sulla fede* in this book are drawn from the *New Blackfriars* version.
3. Johnson's words are quoted by John Wilkins in his article 'Soldiers or pilgrims?', *The Tablet*, 22 November 2003.
4. ibid.
5. Joseph Ratzinger, *Introduction to Christianity* (Crossroad, 1969).
6. The text of this lecture is obtainable from the Eternal Word Television Network, 5817 Old Leeds Road, Irondale, AL 35210, USA.
7. The disclosure was made in conversation with the German journalist Peter Seewald.

1: Boyhood

1. Joseph Ratzinger, *Milestones: Memoirs, 1927–1977* (Ignatius Press, 1998), p. 8.
2. Nicholas Boyle, *The Tablet*, 7 May 2005.
3. ibid.
4. See John Cornwell, *Hitler's Pope: The Secret History of Pius XII* (Viking, 1999), especially chapters 5–9. Some of Cornwell's arguments are over-pitched, but his main thesis is reliable.
5. Ratzinger, *Milestones*, p. 15.
6. ibid., pp. 19–20.
7. John L. Allen Jr, *Cardinal Ratzinger: The Vatican's Enforcer of the Faith* (Continuum, 2002), pp. 17–21.
8. Ratzinger, *Milestones*, p. 26.

9. ibid., p. 27.
10. ibid., p. 32.
11. ibid., p. 37.

2: Studies
1. Ratzinger, *Milestones*, p. 52.
2. ibid., p. 59.
3. ibid., p. 56.
4. ibid., p. 57.
5. ibid., p. 99.
6. ibid., p. 101.
8. *The Times Literary Supplement*, 7 February 2003.
9. *Milestones*, p. 109.
10. ibid., p. 112.
11. ibid., p. 114.

3: Vatican II in Actuality and Retrospect
1. Nicholas Lash, in an interview with the author (May 2005).
2. John Wilkins, 'Earthquake in Rome', *The Tablet*, 12 October 2002.
3. Ralph M. Wiltgen, *The Rhine Flows into the Tiber: A History of Vatican II* (Hawthorne Books, 1967).
4. Giuseppe Alberigo and Joseph A. Komonchak (eds.), *A History of Vatican II* Vol. 2 (Orbis, 1997), p. 69. See also Joseph Ratzinger, *Theological Highlights of Vatican II* (New York, 1966), p. 5.
5. *Concilium*, Vol. 1 (1965), p. 30.
6. Ratzinger, *Milestones*, p. 120.
7. ibid., p. 128.
8. ibid., p. 128.
9. ibid., p. 123.
10. ibid., pp. 123–4.
11. The group's website is www.ecclesiadei.org (last accessed September 2005).
12. Joseph A. Komonchak SJ, 'The Church in Crisis: Pope Benedict's Theological Vision', *Commonweal*, 3 June 2005.
13. These words (quoted in Komonchak's article) come from Ratzinger's commentary on *Gaudium et Spes* in Herbert Vorgrimler (ed.), *Commentary on the Documents of Vatican II*, Vol. 5 (Herder and Herder, 1969), p. 119.
14. Ratzinger, *Milestones*, p. 133.
15. ibid., p. 135.

4: Jumping Ship
1. Rowan Williams, 'Barth and Balthasar', in John Riches (ed.), *The Analogy of Beauty* (T&T Clark, 1986).
2. Ratzinger, *Milestones*, p. 137.
3. Christoph Schwöbel, in an interview with the author (May 2005).
4. Gerald O'Collins, in an interview with the author (May 2005).

5. Ratzinger, *Introduction to Christianity*, p. 116.
6. ibid., p. 91.
7. More of Fessio's reflections on Pope Benedict can be read online by visiting www.ignatiusinsight.com (last accessed September 2005).
8. ibid., p. 143.
9. ibid., p. 143.
10. ibid., p. 144.
11. ibid., p. 148.
12. Joseph Ratzinger, *Eschatology: Death and Eternal Life* (Catholic University of America Press, 1988), p. 59.
13. Aidan Nichols OP, *The Thought of Benedict XVI: An Introduction to the Theology of Joseph Ratzinger* (Continuum, 2005), p. 168.
14. Ratzinger, *Eschatology: Death and Eternal Life*, p. 191.
15. Ratzinger, *Milestones*, p. 155.
16. The text of Rahner's letter appeared in the *Süddeutsche Zeitung* on 14 November 1979.
17. Hans Küng, *My Struggle for Freedom* (Continuum, 2003).
18. The episode was recalled in Hume's obituary in *The Tablet*, 26 June 1999.
19. ibid.

5: The Prefect's Project: An Overview

1. Joseph Cardinal Ratzinger, *Salt of the Earth: The Church at the End of the Millennium* (Ignatius Press, 1997), p. 92.
2. Fergus Kerr OP, 'The Cardinal and post-conciliar Britain', *New Blackfriars*, June 1985, p. 299.
3. Jacques Dupuis SJ, *Toward a Christian Theology of Religious Pluralism* (Orbis, 1999).
4. This comment and related material can be read on the personal website of Dr Ingrid Shafer, or by visiting www.ecumene.org (last accessed September 2005).
5. See Allen, *Cardinal Ratzinger*, p. 272ff.
6. Robert Nugent (ed.), *A Challenge to Love: Gay and Lesbian Catholics in the Church* (Crossroad, 1983).
7. Lisa Sowle Cahill, *America*, 14 August 1999.
8. Ratzinger, *Salt of the Earth*, p. 133.
9. ibid., p. 209.
10. Francis Sullivan SJ, 'Heresy and women priests', *The Tablet*, 18 January 1997.
11. Ratzinger, *Salt of the Earth*, p. 210.
12. Ratzinger, *Rapporto sulla fede*, as translated in *New Blackfriars*, p. 269.
13. ibid., p. 269.
14. Leonardo Boff, *Church: Charism and Power – Liberation Theology and the Institutional Church* (Crossroad, 1986).
15. Francis McDonagh, 'The problem of the poor', *The Tablet*, 18 September 2004.
16. Terrence Merrigan, reviewing Dupuis' 'Christianity and the Religions:

From Confrontation to Dialogue', *The Tablet*, 9 August 2003.
17. Jacques Dupuis SJ, 'The storm of the Spirit', published in *The Tablet*, 20 October 2001.

6: Controversialist and Apologist
1. As indicated above, quotations from the interview on which this book is based are taken from the translation of the Italian original made for *New Blackfriars*.
2. Joseph Cardinal Ratzinger, *God and the World: A Conversation with Peter Seewald* (Ignatius Press, 2002).
3. Ratzinger, *God and the World*, pp. 13–15.
4. *New Blackfriars*, p. 263.
5. Rozier's remarks were reported in *The Tablet*, 10 August 1985.
6. ibid.
7. 'Seeking a new balance', *The Tablet*, 14 December 1985.
8. See Peter Hebblethwaite, 'The mind of Walter Kasper', *The Tablet*, 19 October 1985.
9. Kerr, *New Blackfriars*, p. 299ff.
10. Eamon Duffy, 'Urbi but not orbi . . . the Cardinal, the Church, and the World', *New Blackfriars*, p. 272ff.
11. Nicholas Lash, *New Blackfriars*, p. 279ff.
12. John Mahoney SJ, *New Blackfriars*, p. 288ff.
13. Ratzinger, *Salt of the Earth*, pp. 237–8.
14. ibid., p. 94.
15. ibid., p. 94.
16. ibid., p. 95.
17. ibid., pp. 96–7.
18. Ratzinger, *God and the World*, pp. 13–14.
19. ibid., p. 15.
20. ibid., p. 18.
21. ibid., p. 19.
22. ibid., p. 22.
23. ibid., p. 22.
24. ibid., p. 23.
25. ibid., p. 31.
26. ibid., p. 408.
27. ibid., pp. 429–30.
28. ibid., p. 402.
29. ibid., p. 442.
30. ibid., p. 460.

7: The Turn of the Screw
1. Joseph Ratzinger, *The Nature and Mission of Theology* (Ignatius Press, 1995).
2. George Weigel, *Witness to Hope: The Biography of John Paul II* (HarperCollins, 1999), p. 387.

3. Ladislas Orsy SJ, 'Power to the bishops', *The Tablet*, 7 July 2001.
4. See, for example, Miroslav Volf, *After Our Likeness: The Church as the Image of the Trinity* (Eerdmans, 1997), pp. 71–2.
5. See Robert Leicht, 'Cardinals in conflict', *The Tablet*, 28 April 2001.
6. ibid.
7. ibid.
8. See *The Tablet*, 17 January 1998.
9. Paul Zulehner, 'Deaf to the faithful', *The Tablet*, 17 March 2003.
10. ibid.
11. ibid.
12. See *The Tablet*, 10 July 1999.
13. See the *National Catholic Reporter*, 10 September 1999.
14. Joseph Cardinal Ratzinger, *The Spirit of the Liturgy* (Ignatius Press, 2000).
15. See, for example, the review by John F. Balvodin SJ in *America*, 7 May 2001.
16. Ratzinger, *God and the World*, p. 416.
17. Christopher J. Walsh, 'Minding our language: issues of liturgical language arising in revision', a paper for Ceiliúradh, Dublin, 20 June 2000.

8: The German Shepherd

1. It has been suggested, for example, that by 2003, John Paul did not know the location of St John Lateran (Rome's cathedral), and did not recognise the Archbishop of Canterbury when Dr Williams visited him in October of that year. See John Cornwell, *The Pope in Winter: The Dark Face of John Paul II's Papacy* (Viking, 2004), p. 267.
2. John L. Allen, *The Rise of Benedict XVI* (Penguin, 2005), Chapter 4.
3. See, for example, *The Tablet*, 23 April 2005.
4. Anthony Burgess, *Earthly Powers* (Penguin, 1980), Chapter 68.
5. *The Tablet*, 23 April 2005.
6. ibid.
7. Margaret Hebblethwaite, 'The reconciler reaches out', *The Tablet*, 30 April 2005.
8. Robert Mickens, 'From the Tiber to the Rhine', *The Tablet*, 27 August 2005.
9. Robert Mickens, 'The Thomas Reese affair', *The Tablet*, 14 May 2005.
10. Rowan Williams, Hay Festival Lecture, 2002. The Archbishop's text is available online in the archive of www.hayfestival.co.uk (last accessed September 2005).
11. Joseph Ratzinger, *Church, Ecumenism and Politics* (Hyperion, 1996).
12. Aidan Nichols OP, 'Joseph Ratzinger's theology of political ethics', *New Blackfriars*, September 1987, p. 384.
13. Nicholas Boyle, 'On earth, as in heaven', reproduced in *The Tablet*, 9 July, 2005.

Index

Index

Index